Remaking the Song

ƐB
CB

The Ernest Bloch Professorship
of Music and the Ernest Bloch Lectures
were established at the University of California
in 1962 in order to bring distinguished figures
in music to the Berkeley campus from time to time.
Made possible by the Jacob and Rosa Stern
Musical Fund, the professorship was founded
in memory of Ernest Bloch (1880–1959),
Professor of Music at Berkeley
from 1940 to 1959.

THE ERNEST BLOCH PROFESSORS

1964	Ralph Kirkpatrick
1965	Winton Dean
1966	Roger Sessions
1968	Gerald Abraham
1971	Leonard B. Meyer
1972	Edward T. Cone
1975	Donald Jay Grout
1976	Charles Rosen
1977	Alan Tyson
1980	William Malm
1981	Andrew Porter
1982	Ton De Leeuw
1983	James Haar
1985	Richard Crawford
1986	John Blacking
1987	Gunther Schuller
1988	George Perle
1989	László Somfai
1993	Susan McClary
1994	Wye J. Allanbrook
1995	Jonathan Harvey
1997	Lydia Goehr
1998	Izaly Zemtsovsky
1999	David Huron
2002	Roger Parker

Remaking the Song

*Operatic Visions and Revisions
from Handel to Berio*

Roger Parker

UNIVERSITY OF CALIFORNIA PRESS

Berkeley   Los Angeles   London

The publisher gratefully acknowledges the generous contribution to this book provided by Edmund and Jeannie Kaufman as members of the Literati Circle of the University of California Press Foundation.

University of California Press, one of the most distinguished university presses in the United States, enriches lives around the world by advancing scholarship in the humanities, social sciences, and natural sciences. Its activities are supported by the UC Press Foundation and by philanthropic contributions from individuals and institutions. For more information, visit www.ucpress.edu.

University of California Press
Berkeley and Los Angeles, California

University of California Press, Ltd.
London, England

Library of Congress Cataloging-in-Publication Data

Parker, Roger, 1951–.
    Remaking the song : operatic visions and revisions from Handel to Berio /
Roger Parker.
        p.   cm. — (Ernest Bloch lectures)
    Includes bibliographical references and index.
    ISBN 0-520-24418-4 (cloth : alk. paper).
    1. Operas.   2. Music—Philosophy and aesthetics.   I. Title.   II. Ernest Bloch
lectures.

ML1700.P37   2006
782.1—dc22   2005020676

Manufactured in the United States of America

15 14 13 12 11 10 09 08 07 06
10 9 8 7 6 5 4 3 2 1

The paper used in this publication meets the minimum requirements of ANSI/NISO Z39.48–1992 (R 1997) *(Permanence of Paper)*.

To Lynden

Take any literary work, preserve its semantic—even its doc-umentary—identity as best you can, and then track its changes of meaning as it passes through the attention of dif-ferent places, times, circumstances. . . . We still often seem to think that art's multiple meanings are a function of some-thing they possess on their own, inherently or essentially as it were. But the truth is that meanings multiply, like people, through intercourse.

—Jerome McGann, *Byron and Romanticism*

It would be a travesty to say that Guy suspected Apthorpe of lying. His claims to distinction—porpoise-skin boots, a high-church aunt in Tunbridge Wells, a friend who was on good terms with gorillas—were not what an imposter would invent in order to impress. Yet there was about Apthorpe a sort of fundamental implausibility. Unlike the typical figure of the J[udging] D[istance] lesson, Apthorpe tended to become faceless and tapering the closer he approached.

—Evelyn Waugh, *Men at Arms*

The friends that have it I do wrong
Whenever I remake a song,
Should know what issue is at stake:
It is myself that I remake.

—W. B. Yeats

CONTENTS

PREFACE AND
ACKNOWLEDGMENTS

These days one needs to be careful. The acknowledgments used to be a safe haven: a place where matters both personal and professional could be uncomplicated and mixed; in which—to paraphrase Nabokov—tributes to Professor Advice, Professor Encouragement, and Professor Every Assistance could mingle freely with humbler gestures of gratitude to simple friends and complicated sustainers. But now, quite possibly encouraged by the elaborate personal revelations some have been emboldened to display within their writings, reviewers can enter the garden with swords unsheathed. One of my predecessors as Ernest Bloch Lecturer began her monograph with a generous preface that received this very treatment at the hands of a critic: in my opinion one heavily laden with unspoken agendas. The same might happen here. But what to do? I resist turning these paragraphs into something entirely scholarly; something that judges distance; something that could if necessary be defended.

I do so because, first of all, I want to record unambiguously that this book owes its existence to an extraordinary institutional environment, peopled by an extraordinary group of scholars. The entire project was in this sense a collaborative venture from the start. I spent a total of four months in Berkeley during the fall of 2002, and there I gave the six Bloch lectures that became the six chapters of this book. Three of them (chapters 2, 4, and 6) had existed in previous incarnations but were substantially refurbished to suit their new situation; the others were created there and then. To put this more bluntly, I sat down most mornings during those four months in Berkeley, inspired by the sunshine and the view from a beautiful house near the Claremont Hotel, and I tapped into my computer most of this book. After a month of acclimatization and library haunting, I walked at two-week intervals down Ashby, up College, and into the Music Department; and there I read out such pages as had appeared. In these circumstances the presence of my interlocutors, of a very particular and largely unchanging audience, was ever with me and guided in important ways the shape and tone of what emerged.

This book, then, bears many traces of its circumstances; but one in particular is worth elaboration. Although the chapters range widely in operatic subject matter, they are linked by a common theme, one quite forcefully announced in the first chapter and in no need of repetition here. My principal difficulty in writing the rest was, as I saw it, to create difference—rhetorical difference between the various chapters, of course, but also a sense of progression. My principal fear was one of implosion, that conclusions would begin to fall into each other. To steal a phrase from Arrigo Boito (discussing *Falstaff*), I feared that moment when the audience knows it's all over, but when the action has nevertheless to continue on stage. The lecturer stands alone with his unchanging sheets of paper, obliged to drone through a series of rhetorical moves that he knows have been predicted by his too-attentive listeners. Whether I have succeeded in avoiding this pitfall (one, let's face it, not unfamiliar to people of academic inclination) is of course for others to say; but whatever merits the book can claim in this direction are bound up with the presence of those interlocutors—a group of people with whom I discussed the project, sometimes formally, sometimes in various stages of scholarly undress, on an almost daily basis. These discussions did more than just enrich my enfeebled first thoughts; crucially, they took me away from my narrow, imploding concerns; they encouraged me to read further, listen harder, think again.

How to name all these people? I have to be summary. Thanks, then, to Carolyn Abbate, who of course read the entire typescript, and whose gentle, lucent traces are scattered in many likely and unlikely places; Wendy Allanbrook, who had the courage to be passionate about her Mozart; Albert Ascoli, who read Romani for me; Bill Ashbrook, whose humane Puccini made mine more possible; Suzanne Aspden, who led me by the hand through Handel; Laura Basini, who finished her Verdi as mine rolls on, and whose sheer goodness of heart made plain many rough places; Karol Berger, who was skeptical about "leitmotivic" certainties; Kathy Bergeron, who (always) reads with the acutest of ears; Luciano Berio, whose interest creatively unnerved me; Daniel Brownstein, who was patient of invasions; Stefano Castelvecchi, whose Mozart library became mine, and who then remained calm; Martin Deasy, who has fallen among Donizettians; Nathne Denis, who was my PE guru; Gabriele Dotto, who helped access a composer's authority; Kathy and William Fitzgerald, who endlessly renegotiated the transatlantic divide; Hannah Ginsborg, who changed chapter 1, in the process making me wish I had read more philosophy; Heather Hadlock, who shared endless Palo Alto coffee and sympathy; Dan Heartz, who gave me offprints and was kind enough not to question me too closely; Karen Henson, whose readings turned an old table; Stephen Hinton, who explained editing chez Kurt Weill; Linda and Michael Hutcheon, who launched chapter 4 on the best possible course; Andrew Jones, who lent me his Handel scholarship even when he must have sensed my purpose; Linda Kerber, who sent me a touching e-mail just after chapter 2's 9/11-tinged premiere; Joe Kerman, whose ear and wit are sharper than ever; Gundula Kreuzer, who loved Berkeley as much as I did; Tom Laqueur, whose confusion made me draft chapter 1 more radically; Christine Lucia, who drove me to Fort Hare and back, and who made the imaginative leap; Winfried Ludemann, who presided over chapter 6's Cape Town premiere; Roberta Marvin, whose invitation to Iowa started off chapter 2, and whose hospitality after The Event was heroic; Davitt Moroney, whose blasts from the distant and sometimes personal past were sometimes heeded; Roger Moseley, who reluctantly permitted hints of his well-hidden genius to emerge; Mavis Noluthando Mpola, whose singing miraculously made a 5,000-mile connection; Tony Newcomb, who patiently led Schumann and other distant Germans into the ring; Michel Noiray, who battled heroically with the BNF; Kate van Orden, who offered horse cultural and other asides; Pierluigi Petrobelli, who stands quietly at the back of everything I write; Hilary Poriss, who generously shared when our paths crossed; John Roberts, who tried to keep me honest about Handel and many formal matters; Arman Schwarz, who shared his embarrassingly greater knowledge of Berio; Emanuele Senici, who is always on hand to keep my Italian half-decent, and who read the entire typescript with care and imagination; Mary Ann Smart, who resides, now serenely, at the center of my Berkeley, and who as always read every word; John Spitzer, who told me about Rossini in the Xerox room; Frances and Randy Starn, who were models of hospitality and who remain master/mistress of the wine-fueled intellectual exchange; Richard Taruskin, who wrote an entire article about my topic but was generous enough to cede territory to an interloper; Marco Uvietta, who made the hard yards with Berio's *Turandot*.

Finally I want to thank Lynden Cranham, who was my constant Berkeley companion. As I sat below, tapping and typing, she sat above, playing Beethoven cello sonatas in preparation for what would be an extraordinary concert at Stanford. The trace of this aural background to the project is so great that, many months later as I write these lines, themes from Op. 69 edge onto my mental soundtrack. Lynden did, though, put down her bow for long enough to attend the first lecture: so far as either of us could remember (this after thirty-five years of cohabitation) it was her first exposure to musicological discourse, whether mine or anyone else's. The fact that she then came back to hear the other five was, by my lights, quite beyond the call of duty. Careers bump along partly by means of such unexpected gestures; the cumulative effect is, as they say, something quite other.

Cambridge-Havant, 2004

ONE

Remaking the Song

Those who wish to abolish death (whether by physical or meta-physical means)—at what stage of life do they want it to be halted? At the age of twenty? At thirty-five, in our prime? To be thirty-five for two years sounds attractive enough, certainly. But for three years? A little dull, surely. For five years—ridiculous. For ten—tragic.

The film is so absorbing that we want this bit to go on and on . . .

You mean, you want the projector stopped, to watch a single motionless frame? No, no, no, but . . . Perhaps you'd like the whole sequence made up as an endless band, and projected indefinitely? Not that, either.

The sea and the stars and the wastes of the desert go on for-ever, and will not die. But the sea and the stars and the wastes of the desert are dead already.

—Michael Frayn, *Constructions*

I will start with a personal confession: one that readers will be pleased to know is among very few in this book. There have been times recently, in our new century, my life much more than half over, when I have found myself bored by *La bohème*; when I have merely sighed at the prospect of another *Aida*; when, shame of shames, I have been less than eager for the latest *Figaro*. These works, together with the hundred or so other stal-warts we call the operatic repertory, have sustained both saints and sin-ners through a century and more of operatic history, a century and more that have seen a precipitate decline in new operatic works, and hence an inevitable narrowing of the fare on offer.[1] In spite of the fact that I have shown an intense, sometimes obsessive concern for many of these stalwarts, the energy that fuels my repertory has been getting low. I am here to argue for change.

When it comes to the operatic repertory, change is of course nothing new. Those hundred or so full members of the club have not, as some are prone to think, maintained their presence over a century of music making simply by means of some numinous artistic force radiating from them: on the contrary, they have been kept on the road, and in more or less healthy condition, by means both many and varied. Most obviously they are sustained through the agency of performers: through the energies and human vulnerability of singers and (more recently) conductors. We measure our evolving responses to these canonic works above all through the impact that performers can make in them and on them. There are many subtle pleasures to be taken here. If we are lucky, we will often experience how a singer's transient gifts inscribe themselves on our repertory, causing new connections to be formed, new ways in which we hear afresh works we thought we knew everything about.[2]

Let me offer an example. In the summer of 2002 I went obsessively, black tie and all, to Weber's *Euryanthe* at Glyndebourne in England; and I returned again and again, at some peril to my bank balance, because I became aurally fixated on Anne Schwanewilms, who was singing the title role.[3] I had heard her as Leonore in *Fidelio* the year before, and something in her voice (I don't know how to describe it—perhaps as a highly individual mixture of power and vulnerability? certainly a "something" more visceral than intellectual) kept her music in my mind for days and then weeks afterward. Hearing her again, in *Euryanthe*, at first constructed a miraculous bridge to that Leonore of the past: a small box opened and I had access to those evenings at *Fidelio*, ones that had otherwise long disappeared, inevitably superseded by more immediate musical sensations. But Schwanewilms's *Euryanthe* had now also taken up residence, and for much of the summer the two operas rattled around in my head; intellectual, potentially even musicological connections between them sprang up and were carried along on a thread of vocal timbre. Now, of course, *Euryanthe* is itself long in the past, the physical impact of Schwanewilms's voice has again inevitably faded. I comfort myself by thinking about her Ariadne or her Arabella, her imagined timbre creating further connections between otherwise quite separate works. Maybe she'll come back to Glyndebourne as one of these Strauss heroines; and if she does the fading moments of *Euryanthe* may reappear, Strauss and Weber coming into contact—a transient sound building bridges between the past and the future, in the process shifting my relationship to the musical material it has touched.

As the belletristic swerve of those last sentences too aptly illustrates, it's hard to describe the ways in which performers affect our perceptions of musical works—hard, at least, to write about them in scholarly terms likely to be of more than passing interest to others. And so, although a few individual singers play a role in what follows, I will for the most concentrate on other, more easily definable ways in which that gaudy potpourri we call the operatic repertory changes as it is repeatedly brought into being. As new operas started to dry up during the second half of the nineteenth century, the then-hardening repertory began to compensate by expanding backward, the idea of the "first modern performance" (of early Verdi, of Gluck, of Mozart, of Handel) smoothly substituting for the idea of the "world premiere." A little later, first in Germany and then elsewhere, came the phenomenon of *Regieoper*, the habit of aggressively updating the visual embodiment of old works. This technology-fueled innovation, which was also linked to developments toward abstraction in the fine arts, seems to have started life as an attempt to make unfamiliar operas in now-forgotten idioms relevant to modern audiences. But it soon became, and has notoriously remained, a way of refreshing or problematizing repertory works that were otherwise judged too well known.[4] Later still came the idea of "historical performance," which (as Richard Taruskin has not tired of telling us) also attempted to defamiliarize the all-too-familiar object, added a patina of newness or modernity that, although it claimed identity with the past, was no more than superficially different from the efforts of those self-styled modernizing stage directors.[5] More recently, further commodifications of the operatic object have emerged, ones typically carrying with them new claims for authenticity and, with these, new financial and artistic demands. Old operas are now launched in new editions, which may promise for the first time unimpeded access to the composer's voice; or in "original versions," which may boast of a shape untouched by the world's reception, returning us (we are assured) to a time before the work became a common object of desire. Open the door of the opera house today and you might be greeted with a version of Verdi's *Don Carlos* so complete that it contains items cut during rehearsals for the premiere and never performed in the composer's lifetime; or perhaps a hypothetical restoration of the same composer's *Gustavo III*—an imagining of what he might have written had the censors not insisted that *Un ballo in maschera* translate from scary, regal Sweden into, of all places, seventeenth-century Boston.

I should say straight off that I welcome the spirit of all these endeavors, all these ways in which the operatic repertory has been and is being refigured. And my welcome remains despite my sometime exasperation at the results: at self-indulgent (and self-important) stage directors or at slavishly literal historical performers; at the claims for exclusive authority that can attend the rhetoric of both these groups; at the efforts of incautious, attention-seeking editors (the "finally you will hear *Figaro* as Mozart really wanted it" type of claim). I bear these occasional tribulations with patience because I know that the repertory—so plainly, so inescapably part of our modern condition—needs to evolve, needs to adapt to our changing human situation, if it is to continue to challenge us. As I said, part of that process obviously comes from without; from the (often temporary) addition of new or rediscovered works, and the (sometimes temporary) falling away of others. But it is the more inward process that will primarily interest me in this book: the way constituent members of the repertory alter gradually over time. While this inner transformation has certainly occurred during our recently departed century, I want to suggest that it has done so in an unnecessarily restricted way, overwhelmingly in the domains of staging and instrumental performance. I want, in short, to explore the possibilities of going further; and that *further* will involve alterations to the music.

With that last sentence I may for some have crossed into the realm of the unspeakable. Those who seek to denigrate modern directors of old operas often, for example, fling at the objects of their scorn what they assume to be a reductio ad absurdum. OK, they say, you've set *The Marriage of Figaro* in Elvis Presley's Graceland. Then why don't you use electric guitars instead of Mozart's orchestra? Why not add in a few of the King's greatest hits? Why, in other words, not tamper with Mozart's music as freely as you tamper with the staging?[6] These questions are meant to be triumphantly rhetorical: they are assumed to have no answer because they invoke something "we all" regard as untouchable; after all, Mozart's music, perhaps his late operas in particular, are among the most powerful cultural symbols of our recent past. In striking this pose, the rhetorical questioners set conveniently to one side (or perhaps simply deem irrelevant) a number of historical circumstances: that their stern attitude to the untouchability of musical texts has its own history, and one of comparatively recent making; that Mozart's (and everyone else's) operas were routinely adapted during his lifetime and long after to suit local conditions and tastes; that Mozart himself was at times a willing helper in this process, adding freely to his own works and those of others. So a part of my task in what follows is precisely to bring these and other disturbing historical circumstances to the fore. The questioners' assumption—that there can be no reasoned response to their just rhetoric—suggests a dangerous complacency about their condemnations of people who (in their terms) tamper with the operatic work, in particular with its musical text; if nothing else, I am asking them to think through their prejudices. To put it more bluntly: why *not* also the music?

I am hovering on the edge of large issues here. The authority of the author over his text is of course involved, as is the authority of the work itself, not to mention that old question of where the latter might be located. Discussion of all this in connection with musical works has always been tricky: what is the relation between the score (the material trace) and its various performances? and in which does the work reside? Debates have circled around such notions for centuries, but they have recently been given significant impetus by Lydia Goehr's book *The Imaginary Museum of Musical Works*, first published a decade ago.[7] Goehr's central claim can be simply stated in her own terms: she submits that "given certain changes in the late eighteenth century, persons who thought, spoke about, or produced music were able for the first time to comprehend and treat the activity of producing music as one primarily involving the composition and performance of works."[8] This claim is, as one might expect, liberally graced with caveats (that "primarily" in the quotation above is perhaps the first of them), but it has nonetheless awakened strong responses in the musicological community—mostly, I think, because by historicizing the idea of the "musical work," by giving it such a local habitation and name, Goehr implicitly suggests that it might not always be with us, that its hold on us might not be as absolute as many have assumed. Some of her respondents were eager to grasp this iconoclastic inference: they may even have wanted to celebrate the idea of a brave new work-less or work-weakened world, finding the whole concept of little relevance to their particular repertories. In one chapter of what amounts to a book-length review of *The Imaginary Museum*, the popular-music historian Richard Middleton, for instance, greeted with some satisfaction "the authority of this system apparently imploding in the late twentieth century."[9] But others saw grave dangers. Reinhard Strohm, one of Goehr's sternest critics (he accuses her of being both derivative and plain wrong in the location of her watershed period), hinted darkly that there may be a "heavy price to pay for abandoning [the work-concept]."[10]

My book will, alas, have little of substance to contribute to this particular debate. It's partly a matter of personal competence—I am of all things no philosopher. I also shy away because the topic has recently been discussed in an unnecessarily inflationary context, one in which the retention or disappearance of the "work-concept" seems to have been thought both a matter of urgent cultural survival, and something on which musicological debate will have a crucial influence.[11] But there is a further, perhaps more defensible reason for reticence on this issue. Although my sidelining of the work-concept debate cannot be complete, I take some heart from the fact that my topic in this book is operatic works, and that they fit the established patterns (and battle lines) rather ill: it is significant, for example, that opera hardly figures in Lydia Goehr's original thesis.[12] I do, though, need to take account here of one specifically operatic aspect of the issue. In a rare attempt to link opera to her theory, Goehr writes that "since the end of the eighteenth century, opera has come to be conceived in either of two ways: first, as an art-form that synthesizes in Wagnerian style all the arts to form an undifferentiated unity of the sort that existed in Antiquity; second as a derivative or hybrid form of a specifically musical art."[13] While the chronology here is debatable, it is nevertheless true, and significant for my purposes, that views of opera began to change in important ways during the nineteenth century.

It is now generally accepted that before the nineteenth century the genre had for the most part been classified as a subspecies of spoken drama: if the idea of a work-concept is historically applicable to eighteenth-century *opera seria*, for example, it resides overwhelmingly in the production of poets such as Metastasio; his *drammi musicali* were the texts printed, reprinted, and reified in "complete" editions; their numerous fleeting manifestations in this or that musical setting were mostly matters of local moment, easily replaced by other composers in other cities at other times. Even though aspects of this regime remained in force in some areas during the early decades of the nineteenth century (perhaps particularly in the case of Italian serious opera), that century did, as Goehr says, see a gradual consolidation of a changed viewpoint, in which music was more and more thought the dominant element of the work, and in which the status of the librettist as a literary figure experienced sharp decline.[14] We are still living in this new world, and to a large extent it sets the agenda of those who would wish above all to preserve the opera's musical text as something sacred. If nothing else, then, some knowledge of the history of this attitude, or at least some inkling of the fact that the attitude *has* a history, may serve to dampen the religious zeal of the protectors.

But, to repeat, the operatic work has always been a difficult case for the work-concept debate, if only because it is so complicated: to give just one example, opera routinely involves the dictates not of an authorial intention but of multiple (often vigorously competing) authorial intentions. Confronted with this difficulty, I have found that a more fruitful way into the topic is to look closely at some cases in which operatic works have undergone revision, creating what we might call a surplus of signature. Of course, surplus caused by the creator almost invariably occurs in any work whose traces survive in more than one pristine source, and because of this it is often dealt with in summary manner. One version is declared definitive, with competing texts judged inferior either because they precede the definitive (toward which the creator is thought to be striving) or they follow some time after it (the creator is now thought to have become foolish or corrupted or simply enfeebled with age). But these creator-surpluses are only the simplest cases. In opera other creators always have their say; performers often exert considerable power, and practical considerations can confuse the issue still further. Considered at all closely, almost all operas become problem works so far as establishing a definitive text is concerned.

In the pursuit of these matters, more immediately helpful to me than any work in the field of musicology have been some sophisticated essays into the field of romantic poetry. The most obvious port of call might seem to be the writings of Jerome McGann, particularly his idea of using electronic media to expand our experience of texts, and of what might be available in a "critical" edition. However, while it is obvious that McGann's notion of a text-expanding universe is related to mine, and probably fruit of the same intellectual climate, I find his ideas as they might impinge on operatic objects have some troublesome aspects. As it happens, he touches on musical issues in an Internet manifesto called "The Rationale of HyperText," an electronic text that under the circumstances it will be appropriate to treat as representative.[15] One of McGann's examples there discusses a putative new edition of Robert Burns's ballad "Tam Glen." Burns's work, McGann says, "is grounded in an oral and song tradition," which means that "paper editions are incompetent to render that most basic feature of his verse." He then offers us a vision, of

> Burns's work in audial forms [he means, among other things, recorded performances] that allowed one to engage the songs in the same kind of scholarly environment that we know and value in works like the [cloth-bound critical] edition. An environment allowing one to navigate between versions, to compare variants, an environment able to supply the central documents with a thick network of related critical and contextual information that helps to elucidate the works.

This might on the surface sound just my kind of thing; and indeed I have no principled objection to it. But questions immediately arise. Could this (should this) strategy be applied to editions of musical works? Should we, for example, encourage an edition of Verdi's *La traviata* that would strive to make available, and allow navigation between, all traces of all musical performances of the work? To assemble that hypertext in any sense critically (at a minimum, this would mean supplying contextual information about the provenance of the various sources) would enmesh the editor in what I would guess are now—literally—millions of textual events. The entire community of musicologists globally would be occupied for countless years. And that's just *La traviata*. Some might think this as good a way as any of using up musicologists; but most members of the guild would rebel against a lifetime spent chasing such extravagantly impossible objects.

In my search for stimulus from scholars of literature, Zachary Leader's book *Revision and Romantic Authorship* has emerged as a more important force. It explores the conundrums raised by notorious multiple texts among some of the most famous eighteenth- and nineteenth-century British poets.[16] Leader discusses at length what he sees as a continuing preference among critics and other arbiters of taste for original thoughts (what Shelley called the "undisciplined overflowing of the soul") over later revisions, particularly much later ones; and he links this preference—I think rightly, if with occasional special pleading—to the lingering influence of romantic ideas about organicism (a doctrine more easily denied than escaped). Just as important for my purpose, though, Leader examines at some length how these difficult matters are bound up with issues of personal identity:

> To some Romantic authors—to some people—personal identity is single and continuous, something indivisible with which we are born; and memory, as John Locke would have it, is its guarantor. To others, personal identity is a creation, the sum of a series of discrete "selves," both over time and at any one time. When the self is thought of as inherently indivisible and continuous, revision is often seen as a simple matter of refinement and clarification. . . . When the self is thought of as something towards which one works, an aspiration or value rather than something given, revision is as much an attempt to establish personal identity as to reveal it.[17]

My title for and final epigraph to this book, from Yeats's verse in 1908, is plain and unequivocal about the stakes here, but many (perhaps most) authors—and I would want to echo Leader by adding "like many (perhaps most) people"—are more ambivalent, often wanting it both ways. This is hardly surprising and may give us some hint of the issues involved in "tampering" with works, not the least of which are troubling thoughts about what constitutes human identity. How much power should we wield over the objects we have created? Ultimately, how much influence should we have over our *Nachlaß*, our estate, the traces we leave for others to contemplate, manipulate, or ignore after our death?[18]

Given this context, it is hardly surprising that the business of revision becomes most contentious when the unstable works thus created are not fashioned by "the author" but by others, whether near or far, approved or unimagined. As will already be clear, I spend some of the later stages of this book navigating these perilous waters. Again the situation is far from simple, however uninflected one's ideas might be concerning the hegemony of the creative genius, romantic or otherwise. Leader discusses at length, for example, the difficult case of Mary Shelley's *Frankenstein*, in which Percy Shelley's extensive revisions—most of which made it into the published text—have been seen by some feminist critics as a brutal invasion, one such critic stating that: "collaboration forced by a more dominant writer on a less powerful and perhaps unwilling 'partner' is a kind of rape."[19] Others, though, have seen a less simple case, in particular because there is evidence that Mary Shelley herself thought Percy's interventions improved her novel. It is clear that, once we pursue these questions in any detail, ethical as well as aesthetic issues cannot long be avoided.

Charting these issues in literary works offers us, of course, many fascinations difficult to reproduce in operatic contexts, not least the fact that, as in the case of *Frankenstein*, the very theme of the work may have something fundamental to do with the conditions of its creation; or, to put this another way, that the conditions of its creation may "enact" its theme (Leader's chapter on Mary Shelley is revealingly entitled "Parenting *Frankenstein*").[20] But there are compensations for the operatic scholar, perhaps above all in music's contribution to the operatic work: in sound's unruly elective affinities—the way it can attach itself happily to what might at first seem the most unlikely text or plot or character; the flamboyantly multiple interpretive possibilities it can provide. What is more, and more to my purpose, the sheer slipperiness of music's signifying field ensures that the operatic "work" can survive startling transformations and still remain coherent: the amount of difference we can accept, the level of exoticism and irrationality, is constantly invigorating and can be hermeneutically challenging.

What I will try to offer, then, is a series of meditations on (also I hope celebrations of) operatic texts, in particular ways in which operas long known to us have been, and might in the future be, subject to change of one sort or another. It will, I should stress immediately, be a project very much less than iconoclastic; I have set myself some fairly rigorous limits, ones both historical and, often, heavily influenced by the composer in question's agenda and what I can divine of his intentions. These limits, though, are dictated mostly by my competencies and interests, not by the sight of some Rubicon whose banks I dare not cross. Let me put this another way. Although in the third chapter I seek to encourage experiments in which the now traditional text of *Le nozze di Figaro* might be expanded and enriched, replacement of "Voi che sapete" with "Heartbreak Hotel" is not on my agenda; nor do I think such a project is likely to appear on many horizons in the foreseeable future. But my particular (and, I would hazard, a general) lack of interest in this particular substitution does not mean that I feel empowered *automatically* to dismiss it, to pronounce that it could never work in any circumstance. To do so would be to hold that one particular configuration of the text of Mozart's *Figaro*, the one various accidents of history have delivered to us, should be thought inviolate; that performances and other imaginings of the work *must* be condemned if they stray from that text.

I am, I hope, sufficiently aware—colleagues at Berkeley and elsewhere tried nobly to make sure of this—that such a position is not without internal problems, particularly in the issue of setting limits.[21] I will have more to say about this later in the book, but here let me admit that an extreme version of my position on *Figaro* would encourage complete rejection of or blithe disregard for a composer's intention over his work; and this would, if generally espoused, lead to a situation in which there would be nothing to distinguish a "work" from its various interpretations or performances. Such an end, logical though it may be, and important as it may be for the very survival of opera as a phenomenon, is not the brave new world I seek: I have spent too much of my life happily immersed in operatic works, listening to them, attending them in the theater, bending over manuscripts that record their texts (often trying to distinguish precisely what can be gleaned of their composers' intentions). I would prefer instead to establish a responsible position in between: one that denies that there are entirely objective rules for aesthetic appropriateness but that nevertheless resists the view that accords everyone, regardless of experience and knowledge, the right to an equal hearing in making aesthetic claims. There is, in other words, a large expanse of middle ground over which debate is possible, and it is that ground I wish to tread.

My examples through this book will, then, be less than shocking to most: as is proper for someone of my profession, they will typically be grounded in details from the historical past. What I attempt is perhaps best described as a chipping away at some very familiar works—testing places where they were and might still be liable to change, in particular finding new ways we might think about them in their altered circumstances. "Chipping away" sounds, I admit, less than grand—hardly the broad sweep and easy authority expected of an earnest Bloch Lecturer; but it is well to move slowly, surrounded by such puissant cultural artifacts, heavy with the accumulations of time and human investment, not least my own.

The chapters that follow are not arranged chronologically but rather describe a sense of progress away from that first "undisciplined overflowing of the soul": some of them set out to destabilize or problematize what we might know of a composer's intention over his work; others examine some interpretative consequences when it is disregarded. The second and third illustrate this dual purpose. In chapter 2 I look at two Verdi operas, *Il trovatore* and *La traviata*, which because of various accidents of history were premiered within six weeks of each other, and whose periods of composition were thus inevitably intertwined. Certainly on the surface they seem highly individual and are often thought antithetical; but at moments they stray into one another, confounding our sense of their separate fictional worlds. The third chapter, as already mentioned, concerns Mozart and again involves two operas separated in our pantheon; this time they are connected by two sopranos, one long dead, the other very much with us. If looked at closely, this time though the lens of the composer's later revisions, parts of these operas again become strangely entangled, may even seem to be in dialogue with each other. Chapter 4 again focuses on compositional intentions and turns back to Verdi, this time to his very last opera, *Falstaff*. That in some ways deceptively simple work had a difficult and complex genesis, one result of which is that its most problematic scene comes into significant and disruptive dialogue with another "last work," one written some years before by the composer's most famous rival. Chapter 5 takes us nearly to the present day, and to Luciano Berio's bold, radical new completion of Puccini's *Turandot*. Here is an opera that its creator did not live to complete and that thus is fated to have difference embedded within it whenever it takes the stage; how we deal with this difference is itself interesting, but in the case of *Turandot*, and for a variety of reasons, the business of choosing a proper completion might most clearly be seen to have an ethical dimension. The final chapter deals with Handel, all of whose operas were unperformed for much more than a century after his death, but whose operatic music nevertheless retained a hold on musical imaginations during those years of neglect, often in the most surprising of contexts.

With this spirit in mind—of a gradual move away from the first moment of creation—I want to close this first chapter among some early moments in the genesis of a remote, long-forgotten work. Gaetano Donizetti's *Adelia* is an opera about which I have, as it happens, some rather peculiar parenting issues of my own. *Adelia* was first performed in Rome in 1840, had a few revivals in the next decade or so, but then, as did all but a handful of Donizetti's operas, disappeared into the most dense obscurity. More surprising, particularly as it is a work from the composer's maturity, *Adelia*'s prolonged sojourn in history's oubliette survived even the post-Second World War "Donizetti Renaissance," which saw revivals of almost all his later works. Sometime in the 1990s, Gabriele Dotto and I were casting around for new titles to include in the Donizetti critical edition (we are its general editors) and stumbled on an ancient score of *Adelia*. It looked worth reviving. I spent two summers doing a preliminary edition. And so, in 1997, in Donizetti's home town of Bergamo, the opera finally received its first modern performance. It was revived in Genoa in 1998; a CD was released with Mariella Devia in the title role; a New York performance (in 1999, again with Devia) was broadcast widely; in other words, *Adelia* is now out there.[22] It doesn't, for sure, have full membership in the repertory club; but at least it now has a shot at the entrance examination. One might imagine that I felt pleased when "my" opera thus returned to the world stage; but parenting is a hard, above all an unpredictable business. Not long after those first performances, I began to wonder about, even agonize over, what the edition had *not* included.

This mostly happened because I had come across a series of sketch pages for the opera, housed in the Bibliothèque Nationale de France.[23] For those unfamiliar with the Donizetti's working methods, the mere existence of sketch material might seem unlikely, if only because he has the reputation of being almost an automatic writer; how else could he have produced seventy-odd operas in a working life of just over twenty years? In 1842, famously, he announced that *Don Pasquale* had cost him "more than ten days of hard work";[24] and a couple of weeks later, after orchestrating *Pasquale*, he started work on *Maria di Rohan*, confiding that "in twenty-four hours I've done two acts. When the subject pleases, the heart speaks, the head takes flight, the hand writes."[25] Shelley's "undisciplined overflowing of the soul" seems almost too mild by comparison. Even though Donizetti was clearly referring to what were the preliminary drafts of his operas—the vocal lines, instrumental bass, and perhaps important accompaniment figures—the speed is nevertheless remarkable: in a matter of days, the essential musical fabric had been put in place. Small wonder he was anxious that, in the age of high romanticism, of the timeless masterpiece produced after agonies of self-absorption, his compositional "secrets" should not become public knowledge.[26] Small wonder, too, that he was addicted to large cups of strong coffee.

There is no need to describe in detail here the Bibliothèque Nationale document,[27] but figure 1 reproduces the verso of folio 10. At first glance, the sense of semiotic crisis is acute: what *are* all these strange shapes, many of them wordless and without harmonic context? Some decoding is possible with the help of the score. A good deal of the page is taken up with sketches for Adelia's Act 1 cabaletta "Al suo piè cader vogl'io," a preliminary version of which had been scribbled down already on the verso of folio 8. The opening four lines of folio 10v. carry the latter stages of a version. Then on line 5 Donizetti has another try at the aria: as a cue under it (on line 6) he has written the recitative verse that precedes it ("fuggir? fuggir?"), and on line 7 the words "avanti la cabaletta" appear. Line 10 sees the start of yet another version, one that develops some considerable momentum (through line 14). Elsewhere in the document, on folios 3–7 but clearly at a later stage than the jottings on folio 10v., we have a failed attempt to make a full orchestral version of the cabaletta. Yet more revisions can then be found on the autograph score of *Adelia* (housed in the Ricordi archives in Milan). All in all, these various documents present us with at least five discrete versions of the opening of the cabaletta.[28] Example 1 reports just the opening four bars of these five versions. The text, given below, sees a defiant Adelia resolve to beg her vengeful father's forgiveness for the guilty love she still feels for the tenor, Oliviero.

> Al suo piè cader vogl'io;
> Rea d'amor soltanto io sono:
> O m'accordi il suo perdono,
> O m'uccida il genitor.
> Ma il furor in me sia spento,
> Ma perdoni ad Oliviero:
> Ah . . . nell'ultimo momento
> Gli dirò che l'amo ancor.

[I want to fall at his feet; / I am guilty only of love: / Let my father either grant me / His forgiveness, or kill me. / Let his fury be exhausted on me, / But let him forgive Oliviero: / Ah . . . in my final moments / I will say I still love him.]

The brief incipits reported in example 1 chart a remarkable process of change. Apart from the overall rhythmic shape (largely dictated by

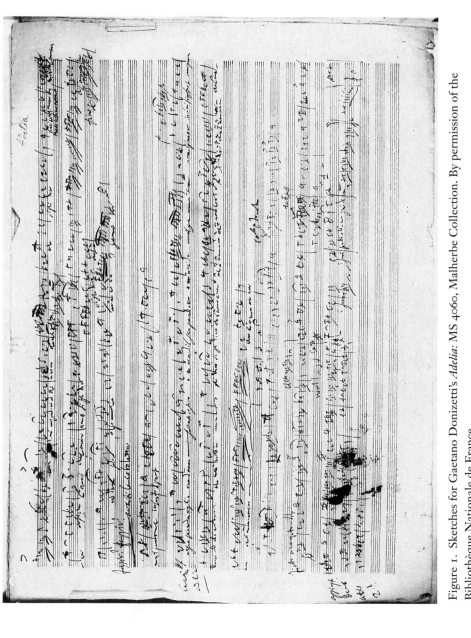

Figure 1. Sketches for Gaetano Donizetti's *Adelia*: MS 4060, Malherbe Collection. By permission of the Bibliothèque Nationale de France.

EXAMPLE 1. Gaetano Donizetti, *Adelia.* Sketches for Adelia's Act I cabaletta "Al suo piè cader vogl'io."

the verse form), two aspects continue throughout: the rise through the octave, further energized by the syncopated rising sixth at the start of bar 2; and an emphasis (hardly surprising in the context) on the word "amor." The first two versions, in D major, are partially without text, as are many of the sketches on these pages;[29] the first two bars are identical, but the remainder is much changed: in version 1 "amor" gets emphasis through a melisma; in version 2, through textual repetition. In version 3 we have moved down a tone, and the first half is given more internal rhythmic energy; but we return in the second half to version 1's solution. Version 4 sees yet another attempt at the second half, this time with "amor" emphasized by a held note and a resolution that keeps the voice in its upper octave. Then comes version 5, the final autograph text, in which the opening two bars are decisively altered, with no vocal lingering on the dominant, and—surprising, perhaps—no falling interval on "cader." The transformations within these opening bars are, I should add, fully characteristic of changes to the rest of the cabaletta, no other part of which remains stable between the various versions. What is more, my story of change could be repeated for other sections of the score, simply on the limited basis of these fragmentary sketches.

What are we to make of all this activity? Could we attach a progress narrative to such remarkable musical proliferation, seeing in the move from version 1 to version 5 a gradual subjugation of crude, "traditional" inspiration by the forces of (forward-looking) artistic virtue? Doubtless it will appeal to some to attempt such a feat. I hope, though, I will offend no one by suggesting that the project will be attended by a hint of desperation. This is not to deny that the changes make a difference. In particular, perhaps, they progressively alter what one might call the directness of utterance: version 5 certainly aids an Adelia who wishes to project force of character much more than does version 1. With just those first four bars before us, such a "progress narrative" might even seem worthy of musicological ink.[30] But the visual context of that entire page of sketches reproduced in figure 1 should surely give us pause; the sheer writerly excess it conveys as note after note, bar after bar, stream onto the page seems peculiarly resistant to rigorous narrative discipline.

I would propose, then, that it is at least as convincing to suggest that, although we can pick a path through them, these sketches also leave us with a sense of something close to sheer proliferation, a joyous pouring forth of difference, an explosion of semiotic *jouissance*, a caffeine-fueled frenzy of creation; above all something that resists easy co-option into an analytical progress-model. Such a reading might initially seem rather defeatist, but it turns out to have important consequences. We know that one of these variants, the last in the chain, version 5, won all the prizes; that my critical edition conferred on it the epithet "definitive"; that it has, by means of this conferment, already inhabited and will now permanently inhabit countless further objects: printed parts, vocal scores, CD recordings, even scholarly monographs. The other versions are destined to remain hidden behind forbidding exteriors, routinely ignored, able to address their voices only to those who from force of philological habit have their ears and eyes straining for different music.

I need to pause. Lest readers think I am carried forth on the wings of postmodern flight, I must immediately step back and remind myself that there is almost everything to be said in favor of this process of natural selection, this last-past-the-post-wins attitude to textual survival. To put the matter at its simplest, no musical work could be performed were that selection not to take place. Nor would I want to claim that Donizetti always, or even habitually, produced sketches that resemble those for Adelia's cabaletta. In many places, on these scattered pages and elsewhere, we can find evidence of what most would agree is purposeful revision, whether because of changed practical exigencies or more abstractly expressive reasons. But those multiple versions of Adelia's cabaletta nevertheless remain before us on this twenty-first-century page. And for me they constitute the first document in an argument. They serve, in short, as a first reminder that it is perilous to be too rigid or too strident about claims for the "authenticity" of an operatic text such as that which reports *Adelia*. Editors can, by following a set of philological rules, indeed marshal the "composer's intention" to their cause; and they are quite proper to do so. But these sketches suggest how fragile that intention might sometimes be, particularly if looked at closely. How would Donizetti have reacted, for example, to an Adelia who strongly preferred version 4 to version 5? Would he have insisted on his *Fassung letzter Hand*, passionately defended its integrity whatever the practical pressure? Or perhaps he changed from version 3 to version 4 because, there in the theater, he heard the voice of Giuseppina Strepponi, the soprano who "created" Adelia, and decided that her low C was getting threadbare. What should the next soprano do, perhaps strong in her low C, perhaps loving version 3's melisma on "amor"?

In the CD recording of "my" *Adelia*, the next soprano is Mariella Devia, and she takes on with some enthusiasm the now-traditional task of ornamenting the literal repeat of this cabaletta; hardly a phrase of Donizetti's original melody goes unaltered, and there are a pair of tremendous high Ds at the close, neither of them carrying a trace of composerly authority. The adding of such embellishments is of course now considered quite legitimate; it is one of the few situations in which per-formers are liable to gather critical praise when they dare alter the musi-cal text, dare leave their personal imprint on an otherwise untouchable aspect of the work. However, elsewhere in the opera, and much more controversially, Devia adjusts the tessitura in some declamatory passages, mostly by using octave transpositions to avoid the lower reaches of the part. Should we condemn this as a distortion of Donizetti's wishes? As far as those wishes are recorded in the final layer of his autograph score, dis-tortion has indeed occurred. But in any larger context, even the context of his sketches, the matter becomes less simple: Devia's "accommoda-tions" might even be seen as an added layer of thoughtful, sensitive inter-pretation of the work. Indeed, I'd go further: if she sings the part again, perhaps I'll show her my sketch material; perhaps one of those rejected versions might inspire her to new variations, new accommodations between her voice and the text Donizetti left us of his opera.

For now, though, Mariella Devia's fearless high Ds at the end of this little-known Donizetti aria, neither of them written by the composer, are pleasure enough. They tell me, after all, that *Adelia* has started another journey even as she arrived on our local scene. We can follow her if we wish, even though we cannot know where or how the journey will end: it will certainly continue long after we all, saints and sinners, are the objects of forgetting. But that is no reason to resist embarkation, to stop the projector on one motionless frame. We can be sure of the fact that, as the journey continues and the landscape changes, we too will alter. Perhaps we will ask new questions, find new meanings in objects we had once thought too familiar to excite us further. Of course, jour-neys can be fraught. The unfamiliar can be unsettling. Identities are at stake: both ours and those of the objects we so happily pursue.

TWO

Of Andalusian Maidens and Recognition Scenes

Crossed Wires in Il trovatore and La traviata

As I was walking, one hot summer afternoon, through the deserted streets of a provincial town in Italy which was unknown to me, I found myself in a quarter of whose character I could not for long remain in doubt. Nothing but painted women were to be seen at the windows of the small houses, and I hastened to leave the narrow streets at the next turning. But after having wandered about for a time without inquiring my way, I suddenly found myself back in the same street, where my presence was now beginning to excite attention. I hurried away once more, only to arrive by another *détour* at the same place yet a third time. Now, however, a feeling overcame me which I can only describe as uncanny, and I was glad enough to find myself back at the piazza I had left a short while before, without any further voyages of discovery.

—Sigmund Freud, "The 'Uncanny'"

TRILOGIA POPOLARE

Rigoletto, Il trovatore, La traviata. I'm not sure who first crowned them the "popular trilogy," but the name, with its suggestion of classical perfection for mass consumption, has ensconced itself in the hall of Verdian critical clichés.[1] Premiered within the space of two years in the early 1850s, these three operas signal an important moment, not only in Giuseppe Verdi's career, but perhaps even in Italian operatic history. As Verdi's popularity waned during the later nineteenth century, all his early operas eventually fell on hard times, then needing—with varying degrees of medical adroitness—to be resuscitated in the twentieth century; but the trilogy obstinately held the global stage. They are among the earliest operas by any composer to have retained a place in the repertory since the moment of their arrival. They have, in other words, never been out of date.[2]

This tendency to group the three works together and then place them in a kind of popular empyrean has frequently led to a further critical move, one that marvels at the seemingly miraculous difference between them. *Rigoletto* and *Il trovatore* are often paired in this way, with the former (form-breaking, recitative-like, unconventional) looking forward into the future, and the latter (all cabalettas and high notes) looking into the past. But the strategy is even more common in the case of *Il trovatore* and *La traviata*, which have often been thought to enfold within them a formidable set of Verdian binaries; epic vs. intimate; public vs. private; conservative vs. radical; romantic vs. realist; even "masculine" vs. "feminine."[3] This is part of what one might call a "universalizing through individualizing" trend in Verdian criticism: a way of suggesting that the operas of the composer's maturity show a well-nigh infinite range (as early as 1859, Abramo Basevi, one of Verdi's most astute early critics, famously talked about a "third manner" arriving with *La traviata*).[4] To put this another way, a significant outlay of critical energy has been devoted to making these works separate from each other. While the early operas are shown to follow shared formulas (and the extent to which they do is often thought an index of their comparative failure), here individuality is all.

The sense of illuminating artistic difference between *Il trovatore* and *La traviata* has generally been judged only the more striking in light of the way the operas are linked in the composer's biography.[5] I need to pause on that tangled history, which has been made much clearer since the publication of both operas in the Verdi critical edition.[6] The essential action occurred during a five-month period at the end of 1852 and the start of 1853. *Il trovatore* had for various reasons fallen seriously behind schedule, this and a lingering illness squeezing the composition of *La traviata* into what was for Verdi an unprecedentedly short space of time. As usual, both operas were created in stages, the first two of which were fundamental to the individuality of the work in progress. First came the parceling up of the subject into operatic forms and the drafting of the libretto (always by this point in his career a collaborative process between Verdi and his librettist); second came the business of musical sketching, which eventually produced a "continuity draft" in which the basic outlines (melody, bass, essential instrumental cues) were written down. The two subsequent compositional stages tended to be more mechanical, although they could be time-consuming and on occasions involved further revisions of existing material, sometimes quite radical ones. First Verdi transcribed the continuity draft onto nested bifolios of manuscript paper (forming a "skeleton score"); and finally he orchestrated the skeleton score, an activity he liked to undertake—at what for us seems alarming speed—after he had arrived at the city of the premiere, during piano rehearsals with the singers.

Just charting this modus operandi as it played out in the case of *La traviata* makes clear the difficulties. With the deadline of his new commission for Venice looming in the early new year of 1853, Verdi and his librettist, Francesco Maria Piave, who was on hand at Verdi's home at Sant'Agata, decided on using the Dumas fils play *La Dame aux camélias* only in mid-October 1852.[7] At that time Verdi was still deep at work on *Il trovatore*, possibly still sketching, possibly just embarked on the skeleton-score stage.[8] In five days in mid-October, Piave roughed out a plot called *Amore e morte* (their draft title for *La traviata*) and then got to work writing the libretto. The timing was tight, but it might have worked had Verdi then not fallen ill with what he described as "rheumatism" in the right arm (was it a form of repetitive strain injury from all the writing and piano playing?), which immobilized him for the best part of a month. By then the situation was parlous. Verdi had to double up on assignments. In mid-November he fell on a desperate plan: he would orchestrate *Il trovatore* while still at home, then travel to Rome (where the *Trovatore* premiere was to take place); during the rehearsal period (when he would normally have orchestrated *Trovatore*) he would sketch out the whole of *La traviata*. In a famous letter, much quoted by early biographers, he asked for a piano to be set up in his Roman apartment.[9]

The plan at first seemed to go well. On the journey to Rome from Sant'Agata, Verdi stopped off in Genoa and later boasted that he had written the first act of *La traviata* there in the space of four days.[10] But then, perhaps inevitably, he became embroiled in the stage preparations of *Il trovatore* and again suffered from "rheumatism." He got some work done, but far less than he had hoped; at one point he despaired of fulfilling his contract with Venice. The *Trovatore* premiere took place on 19 January 1853. Soon after, Verdi traveled back to Sant'Agata and spent the last days of January and the first three weeks of February desperately sketching and producing a skeleton score of *Traviata*. He made it (just), and shot off to Venice on 21 February where, in a little more than two weeks, he orchestrated his new opera, prepared the singers, and made last-minute revisions. The premiere took place on 6 March, barely six weeks after that of *Il trovatore*. It was—the cruelest cut of all—a famous fiasco.

We can see from even this brief account that what I described a moment ago as the most important creative stages of each opera (the planning of the libretto and the sketching of a continuity draft) probably overlapped only a little. The fact remains, though, that in the case of *La traviata* these stages took place during a period in which Verdi was actively involved with *Il trovatore*. During those hectic days on which he was directing Manrico, Azucena, Leonora, and others in Rome, as he heard their music repeated again and again, as it rattled around in his head, he was also struggling to immerse himself in the new fictional and musical world of *La traviata*. As mentioned earlier, this circumstance has in the past merely provided an extra scent for those sniffing out Verdian miracles. How he overcame the petty practicalities of his *anni di galera;* how two such diverse masterpieces could emerge almost simultaneously "proving" the authenticity of his genius. Today, though, it might have other meanings. For one thing, we might conclude that accident and last-minute improvisation, the kind of frenzy of creative outpouring we saw producing Donizetti's *Adelia* in the last chapter, produced *La traviata;* without those unpredictable external events, without stacked deadlines and recurring illness, we can be sure the opera would have turned out quite differently, that a different *Traviata* would be before us. For another, though, there is surely a new angle to pursue in that old binary of *Il trovatore* and *La traviata:* one created not with the grand shapes we have made of nineteenth-century operatic history, but by a strange, unplanned, and altogether unwelcome creative coincidence.

NIGHT VISITORS

We can start, as I did, by pursuing a trail that looks alluring but, at least by the light of modern philology, proves an illusion. The recently published sketches for *La traviata*, documents that will concern me at some length in what follows, might at first glance seem to offer startling evidence of the hectic concatenation of creative projects described above.[11] Fascicle XII of the sketches, as they survive in Sant'Agata to this day, is a single bifolio. Pages 2–4 are taken up with a continuity draft of the start of no. 6, the "Scena Violetta ed Aria Germont" in Act II. Violetta has just finished her duet with Germont, who has departed into the garden; she writes a letter to Alfredo breaking off their liaison and then flees the scene when her lover arrives, singing before she goes the famous, anguished declaration, "Amami Alfredo." Alfredo, left alone, is delivered the letter by a servant, reads it, breaks down in shock and anger; and then—to the dismay of many a critic across the years—is obliged to attend a full-scale double aria sung by his father, who returns just at that moment to comfort him.[12] Sketches for Germont's double aria (the cabaletta of which gave Verdi striking difficulties) are not present in this

fascicle; it was often Verdi's habit to sketch the set pieces of a scene sep-
arately from their surrounding material. Here, then, we have just the
buildup. Drafts such as that found on pp. 2–4 survive for a large part of
the opera and are in no way unusual. But the first page of the bifolio is
quite different: it is occupied by two night visitors. Again the music is
clearly a continuity draft of connective tissue between set pieces, but the
characters taking part are striking a much less sophisticated sexual bar-
gain than did Violetta and Germont: we are in the tempo di mezzo of
the di Luna-Leonora duet in the last act of *Il trovatore*. "M'avrai, ma
fredda, esanime spoglia," groans Leonora: "You'll have me, but as a cold,
lifeless cadaver." What is the sketch doing here? It might immediately
be tempting, following all those *Trovatore/Traviata* binaries mentioned
earlier, to connect these two scenes, to find meaning in their cohabitation on a gathering of sketch paper. At first sight I did so willingly
myself; both scenes, after all, concern a heroine sacrificing herself to a
baritone antagonist in order to "save" her lover. Alas, a love of philology
binds one to a demanding muse: the evidence of the sketches generally,
and of the chronology outlined earlier, suggests that Verdi was doing no
more than using up spare paper when he joined his operas together on
the page in this way.[13] Whether or not that should entirely quash my
efforts to relate the moments is, of course, another matter: perhaps the
shards of connection are like those Anne Schwanewilms created between *Fidelio* and *Euryanthe:* devoid of master plot, antihistorical, but
nonetheless *there*, caused by a very material coincidence.

In this case, though, the spark of recognition set me off on a quite
other course. I soon discovered that if the search is for night visitors
causing strange juxtapositions, there's a more obvious moment of contact, one not buried in sketches but present in the final works for all to
see. Soon after Violetta's moment of pathetic/disgraceful/transcendent
(the appropriate adjective has been much debated recently) female sac-
rifice in *La traviata* comes the opera's great and only scene of public confrontation: Violetta has returned to Paris, taken up with a rival, and
seems to have resumed her Act I, "party" existence; newly jilted Alfredo

tracks her to her friend Flora's house and there publicly insults her. All this is high drama indeed; but the grand scene, which is the finale of Act II, is launched in distinctly Parisian musical style—by a couple of distinctly lightweight divertissements for the assembled sybarites. First come a collection of female partygoers disguised as gypsies (*zingarelle*), then a male group disguised as matadors and picadors. These episodes do not feature in Dumas fils's play and were presumably inserted by Verdi and Piave to stress further the superficial, urban color that is so important to the atmosphere of *La traviata*.[14] In none too clandestine a way, the little stories these masqueraders tell have obvious parallels with the "real" drama. The women read the fortunes of a couple of party guests, playfully detect unfaithfulness, but conclude by suggesting that a veil should be drawn over (mis)deeds of the past. The men then narrate a simple tale of Piquillo, a matador from Biscay, who falls in love with an Andalusian maiden; Violetta-like, the maiden at first sends Piquillo away, but in the song he returns triumphantly to claim her hand. All ends happily ever after, as it has so painfully *not* done for Violetta Valery and Alfredo Germont.

So far, so conventional, one might think. But given the chronological proximity of *Il trovatore*, and of that opera's unrelievedly dark treatment of similar dramatic types, the presence of these standard-issue, tambourine-banging gypsies and other exotics might seem an odd, or at least a noteworthy choice. All the more so, though, when one considers the shared musical contexts. The music that introduces *La traviata*'s mock *zingarelle* (example 2a) is so close as to be almost a recomposition of Ferrando's famous description of the gypsy Azucena in Act I of *Il trovatore* (example 2b); and the latter is related (how closely might depend on one's analytic-motivic zeal) to a further collection of E-minor melodies associated with the "outsider" half of the *Trovatore* plot (examples 2c–d, from Act II; and example 2e, from Act III).[15] Musically, it's as if characters have wandered in from the earlier opera: their brief journey may have necessitated a steep generic change, from "real" gypsies to "stage" caricatures, a change that is brought to the foreground by their

EXAMPLE 2. Thematic shapes shared between Giuseppe Verdi's *La traviata* and *Il trovatore*.

a. *La traviata*, mock *zingarelle*

b. *Il trovatore*, Act I

c. *Il trovatore*, Act II

d. *Il trovatore*, Act II

e. *Il trovatore*, Act III

almost shared melodies. In an aesthetic climate such as that of the mid-nineteenth century, in which the idea of "originality" was gaining importance in the Italian operatic world, and in which composers were routinely criticized when thought to be repeating themselves, why did Verdi leave us with such an obvious footprint from an earlier work?

The connections do not end there. The second strand of the divertissement, peopled by story-telling matadors, betrays a similar musical pathway back into *Il trovatore*, although here the ancestry is if anything more mysterious. The main narrative episode (example 3a) is a further "recomposition" of material from *Il trovatore*, this time of the duet cabaletta between Azucena and Manrico in Act II (example 3b).[16] Here any obvious meaning behind the link is much harder to find: there is of course a generic Spanishness appropriate to both themes, but the circumstances could hardly be more different. One rather has the impression of a more casual process, perhaps the unconscious infiltration of one opera into the other. This latter sense is quite spectacularly reinforced by a small detail from one of the earliest sketches for *La traviata*. As already mentioned, these divertissements serve as a prelude to (perhaps also a comic foreshadowing of) the much more serious confrontation scene that ensues, the action of which is underpinned by a nervous, repeated orchestral figure (example 4a). The motivic derivation of this from the contrasting, major-mode section of the matadors' narrative (example 4b) is quite obvious, and not that unusual for middle-period Verdi: it might even strengthen the idea (mooted earlier) that the story of Piquillo and his Andalusian maiden offers self-conscious parallels to that of Alfredo and Violetta. But much more interesting for my purposes is Verdi's first try at this theme in his sketches (example 4c). As with several of Verdi's very first ideas, its tonality is quite distant from that eventually used;[17] but what leaps from the page is something different, something that may even border on the uncanny. As can be seen by comparing examples 4c and 4d, the opening rhythm and pitches of this very early sketch are more or less identical to a crucial recurring motive in *Il trovatore*, Azucena's famous idée fixe "Stride la vampa," her obsessive image of the flames that consumed her mother and son.[18] If we are to believe his sketches, then, Verdi first "heard" the Act II finale of *La traviata* through the musical lens of one of the most prominent melodies in *Il trovatore*: one that, what is more, we now think of as indelibly linked to a specific image (the flickering flames that consume Azucena's mind and have destroyed her past).

As long as we confine ourselves to this particular scene in *La traviata*, connections between the operas might be explained (although, for reasons advanced earlier, with some difficulty) as basically generic, to do with a common Spanish-ness that can, after all, be found in other operas, by no means exclusively those by Verdi.[19] Readers may at this stage, though, be exercised by something more basic than these local matters,

EXAMPLE 3.   Thematic shapes shared between Giuseppe
Verdi's *La traviata* and *Il trovatore*.

a. *La traviata*

b. *Il trovatore*, Act II

EXAMPLE 4.   Thematic shapes shared between Giuseppe
Verdi's *La traviata* and *Il trovatore*.

a. *La traviata*

b. *La traviata*

c. *La traviata*, sketch

d. *Il trovatore*

might even be uneasy about where my project tends. Had I been exploring the connections *within* an opera, I would of course be on secure, often-paced epistemological terrain, on paths much covered by Verdians and others. There are good, in some cases overwhelming reasons why the latter mode of inquiry, with its search for recurring themes and other dramatically "significant" musical connections, is so impacted by musicological footsteps. After all, we mostly approach and then consume operas through their plots, through what makes them individual. Yet when we look for connections between works, we are more likely to find reassuringly overarching shapes, generic conventions, what in the Verdi trade are called *solite forme*, abstract means toward understanding.[20] The present case is different. Those gypsies who dance into *La traviata* may sound innocuous enough, as is the fact that a sketch fragment, recently revealed, makes us see a sudden connection between very different pieces of music; but the resonances with *Il trovatore*, when pushed upon, can also set up a kind of double presence that might under certain circumstances seem anything but reassuring. I used the word uncanny to describe the connection a moment ago, and certainly Freud's famous essay could be brought into play, not least because to ponder in depth such doubles, to try to find meaning in them, is perhaps part of the problem. "*Unheimlich* is the name for everything that ought to have remained . . . secret and hidden but has come to light."[21] Freud is quoting Schelling here, and the definition will become a key element in his exploration. But the *Geheimnis* in the case I've outlined is the ghostly compositional double that— worst scenario—may *have* no singular logical meaning. Musical recurrence can, it tells us, resist the hermeneutic, not be subject to narrative logic: it can behave in scary ways.

RECOGNITION

My second series of links between these two curiously entangled operas is yet again different, both in type and in the conclusions that might be drawn. It concerns a scene from the first half of Act III of *Il trovatore*, one not much discussed by commentators, and rarely appearing in excerpts. Azucena has been captured and is interrogated by di Luna and Ferrando. She attempts to dissemble, posing as a simple wandering gypsy, even sketching a "characteristic" narrative song about her search for a lost son, "Giorni poveri vivea." But after one verse of this, the count begins to question her closely about past events, and during the course of this interrogation her true identity dawns on Ferrando, as does her implication in dreadful events that took place many years ago. The fact that she is both the avenging gypsy of a generation earlier and the mother of Manrico is revealed. A furious ensemble cabaletta ends the scene; Azucena's justified dread at the future is answered by savage exultation from the count, Ferrando, and the male chorus.

This is, then, a recognition scene of sorts; and one that, given the notorious complexity of *Il trovatore*'s plot, is of necessity rather full of words. Perhaps for this reason the crucial revelation occurs in an orchestrally dominated *parlante* section, a texture that allows the singers to declaim freely and thus ensure that their words are clearly apprehended.[22] The entire passage, which is given in example 5, lasts for 80 measures of $\frac{3}{8}$, andante mosso, and is neatly divided into two main sections: Azucena's minor-mode "dissembling" narrative about her search for her son, and the recognition scene itself, in the parallel major. At the precise center, dividing the two moments, is the major-mode peroration to the narrative, and at the precise center of that peroration (m. 40) comes the vocal climax of the entire episode, Azucena reaching a high G♯ as she describes the love she nurtures for her son.[23]

It is the second, orchestrally dominated section in which the recognition occurs (it begins at m. 45 of example 5). In terms of large-scale musical movement (in particular the phrase lengths, with that unsettling single bar of accompaniment before the tune) it acts as a ghostly second stanza of Azucena's preceding narrative, something perhaps intensified by the fact that both sections make much of an insistent 6–5 melodic figure. What does this modeling tell us? Perhaps that, despite the intensity and gathering pertinence of the interrogation, Azucena's

EXAMPLE 5. Giuseppe Verdi, *Il trovatore*, Act III, scene 1.

EXAMPLE 5 *(continued)*

(continued)

EXAMPLE 5 *(continued)*

fake characteristic song is scrolling by as a false background.[24] But, secret semantic messages aside, the tone—in this tense, not to say critical context—is strangely nonchalant, even superficial, with those repeated trills and elegant chromatic decorations. And the sense of what I want immediately to call "urban" elegance is emphasized by the orchestration, with the violin and cello playing the melody in octaves.[25] There is also the passage around m. 70 (perhaps *the* moment of recognition, when Ferrando lets out a stifled "Sì!"), in which the tune becomes "stuck," as it were, and after which there is a whole measure of eerie silence before the wheels again turn. The effect comes close to "stage music," music scrolling past in some space implicated with the stage action. But whose space? To put this in what might seem a modish manner, where does this elegant tune, those trills, come from?

There are of course many answers to such questions. One might be to pause on a genealogy of nineteenth-century operatic trills, ponder the way they are often used in double-faced, insinuating contexts (Iago's music is full of them). In Act II of *Siegfried*, for example, there is a "mind-reading" scene in which Mime utters horrible words while the music trills urbanely (representing what he is really saying, since Siegfried and we magically hear the unspoken words in his mind). Within this genealogy, urbane trills become a kind of legible dissimulation: there is a text to say what is underneath, but the coincidence of legible text and inscrutable music both gives comfort—we understand the trills as urbane dissimulation—and removes it.[26]

I could continue, but there is no pressing reason if we can agree that the music of this scene is strange enough for such explanations to become insistent—that this passage seems especially in need of exegetical pressure. What I prefer to do here is address something much more audibly obvious: not where the music "comes from" but where it traveled to after its sojourn in *Il trovatore*. The answer, of course, is directly into one of the primary colors of *La traviata*: the characteristic, "salon" orchestration, the almost obsessive trills that become a prime symbol of Violetta's champagne and tears, her dissembling gaiety (Basevi had a

EXAMPLE 6.   Giuseppe Verdi, *La traviata*, Act I, prelude.

wonderful term for them, *appoggiature trillate*).[27] Indeed, we need think no further than the famous prelude, in which that very orchestration and those very trills announce the drama in that very tonality (example 6).

As surely as those gypsies wandered into *La traviata*, so Violetta seems to have wandered into *Il trovatore*, into a brutal interrogation in time of war. As we know from the chronology sketched out much earlier, it seems unlikely that the motivic traffic moved in that direction. Although there can of course be no such thing as proof, this nonchalant, "urban" idea was probably created first for *Il trovatore* and then, perhaps as that opera was being rehearsed, merely imported into *La traviata*, there to become our first introduction to the central theme of the opera. It is nevertheless tempting, perhaps even pressing, to essay an "interpretation" of such a recurrence (or, as I prefer to think of it, such a numinous anticipation). Surely this particular nexus of connection must *mean* something? Of course, experienced seekers that we are, explanations will always be near at hand. Indeed, one has already been hinted at. That "urban" theme in *Il trovatore* belongs in a complex way to Azucena: it is in part an aural representation of her desperate attempts to deflect attention from her true identity (hence the "dissembling" trills and chromaticism); but it also, insistently, betrays the very source of her anxiety, her consuming love for Manrico. What more natural, then, that it would transform into a passage from the *Traviata* prelude, one that introduces the "theme" of Violetta's consuming love for Alfredo but at the same time clothes it in Violetta's ambiguous "surface," those *appoggiature trillate* that never fail to conjure up her deceiving gaiety? This certainly works on one level; but it's too, too literal. It has in some way muted the strangeness of the recurrence; if accepted, it causes the oddly troubling reverberations of this cross-opera resonance to drift away; it reassures us of shape and coherence and meaning.

ONE HOT SUMMER AFTERNOON

I have more than once referred to Freud's famous essay on "The Uncanny," and it's now time, in what will need to be a fairly long conclusion, to take a step back and, first of all, offer a kind of disclaimer. I would not want to press the notion that the connections exposed here between *Il trovatore* and *La traviata* are "uncanny" according to much more than a superficial reading of Freud's complex and—at least to some extent—professionally self-serving sense. For one thing, it would require no little violence to the musical objects if one were to relate these odd thematic resemblances, or those tambourine-slapping gypsies, or even that innocent, urban interrogation melody, to Freud's gaudy succession of automata and dismembered limbs, of doppelgänger and feet that dance by themselves. But, again as I've mentioned more than once, there is nevertheless something unsettling about these musical "doubles"; or, perhaps better, something unsettling about *contemplating* them. The tone of the affair, then, comes closer to that of my epigraph—Freud's faintly comic, faintly sinister account of his Italian urban stroll, in which his repeated appearances in the red-light district are subject to no subsequent deep reading, no analysis of possibly hidden motives on the part of the narrator; in his personal world, the repressed has no return, at least no overt one. To ask the question again: what, then, can the links between these two operas tell us?

For one thing, finding and then savoring these links can present us with a less *controllable* view of a composer's creative workings, just as did contemplating those Donizetti sketches in my first chapter, perhaps again giving us pause: helping us to look critically at the energy we routinely invest in protecting and promoting the internal "integrity" of musical works. For example, while the proximity of these two operas certainly caused a crossing of creative wires, the crossing seemed often to have occurred at a level of unconscious on which we have little purchase. For practical reasons that we can elaborately document, *Il trovatore* was at the front of Verdi's musical mind as he tried to create *La traviata;* the connections that thus emerged might have been unwelcome, even embarrassing. The discipline of sketch studies, or the larger one of musical analysis, has rarely confronted such matters and might occasionally benefit from doing so: from reminding itself that at certain levels the nature of the creative musical act is not easily domesticated into a tale of scholarly conquest. What one might call this "ear-of-the-beholder" view is, after all, routinely discounted in musicology; there remains a strong, hidden prejudice against subjective or singular experience, which is routinely allied with illogic or caprice, in need of being policed and disciplined from the scene. Anyone who writes a book like this one is, of course, inevitably part of the police force, inevitably enjoys the benefits such discipline provides; but what is lost in the exchange should still be investigated.

What effect, then, might "doubles" such as those scattered through *Il trovatore* and *La traviata* have on our approach to the operatic objects in which they reside? They may in the end prove salutary, may even encourage us to think once again about the whole business of musical resemblance, or cross-references, within and between operas. The appearance of moments of musical sameness can, we know it well, fruitfully connect. Particularly when we find them within famous works, our energies, perhaps attempting to match or trace the energies of the composer, will respond with complex interpretation; and the "deeper" the musical resemblance, the deeper are we encouraged to delve for meaning, to broaden and make more universal our interpretive strategies. There is a powerful pull here; but it is one about which we might occasionally be skeptical.

And so, despite earlier protestations, I will end with Freud quoting Schelling. "*Unheimlich* is the name for everything that ought to have remained secret and hidden but has come to light." As I said, the hidden thing in this case is musical connection that may have no meaning or—better—that resists stubbornly being co-opted to the meaning field that we wish to maintain, to one that keeps these two operas from the "popular trilogy" in binary opposition, housing and containing their difference, making their connections no more than comfortably abstract and formal. Let me put this another, final way. With the professional techniques available in this chapter—the finding of thematic and other relationships, the location of these relationships within narratives both historical and operatic—little effort is required to fashion a fine, rolling conclusion. "And thus we see that . . ." See what? That our special skills can underscore with an enticing glimpse of secret workings, of a glowing *Geheimnis*, the individuality of the operatic work, the sense in which it articulates its difference? In this chapter we are left instead with unanswered questions: what are those gypsies doing there? why does Azucena become Violetta as she reveals her "true" identity?

Strangely enough, and though I still prefer to keep the questions unanswered (or rather, multiply answered), this need not be a gloomy conclusion, another aporia, another throwing up of critical hands in the face of insoluble complexities. And it can avoid this recently fashionable but already tiresome state for a very simple reason. Willful, self-serving, even irreverent as it may seem, I tend to sort performances of *Il trovatore* into genera according to their treatment of the Azucena interrogation;[28] and the incursion of those gypsies is the moment in *La traviata* that I always anticipate with the greatest pleasure. Quite probably the reasons for this odd taxonomy are mostly subterranean, too deeply personal to interest others very much. But some of the pleasure these moments give comes from the fact that their musical gaze is directed out of the opera, into another fictional world that, on another evening in this or that theater, we too might inhabit. It could even happen after a hot summer afternoon wandering the deserted streets of some provincial Italian town; but the encounter with these particular "painted women" will not produce unease so much as happy recognition: that operas can hide inside each other and thus confound us pleasurably.

THREE

Ersatz Ditties

Adriana Ferrarese's Susanna

In the June 2002 issue of *Opera News*, the British opera producer Jonathan Miller gave an interview that, doubtless to the delight of many, raked through the coals of an old controversy.[1] In 1998 Miller had directed Wolfgang Amadeus Mozart's *Le nozze di Figaro* at the Metropolitan, mostly to critical acclaim; but in the *Opera News* interview he confided that he has not been invited back to supervise the past season's revival of the production. He had, he said, been "fired" by the management because of a "set-to" during the original production. This referred to a backstage scandal much reported at the time. The 1998 Susanna, Cecilia Bartoli, had taken it into her mind to alter the "traditional" text of the opera. For a Viennese revival of *Figaro* in 1789, three years after the premiere and around the time he was composing *Così fan tutte*, Mozart accommodated the new Susanna by writing for her two new arias, arias intended to replace "Venite, inginocchiatevi" in Act II and "Deh vieni, non tardar" in Act IV. Bartoli, who is famous for her explorations of little-known repertory, wanted to sing these replacement arias at the Met and sing them she did; Jonathan Miller was not pleased. As he put it in the *Opera News* interview:

> I think I behaved fairly reasonably. I expressed my unease about
> using showy arias that are infinitely less interesting and appropriate

to the drama. These [new arias] are twice as long, and their words have nothing to do with the action. During the first aria, Renée Fleming as the Countess was left dressing Cherubino while Bartoli was down on the front beguiling the audience. . . . I was told by [general manager Joseph] Volpe that I had agreed [to the substitutions], and I said yes, I'd agreed rather in the way that France had agreed in 1939.[2]

In an interview nearer the time, Miller had been more outspoken still:

To be absolutely honest, I hadn't the faintest idea what to do with these pieces. [The second of them] left poor old Bryn [Bryn Terfel, playing Figaro and thus obliged to be visible on stage, spying on Susanna as she sings her fourth-act aria] kicking the wall. . . . If you don't sing "Deh vieni" in the fourth act of *Figaro*, it's like coitus interruptus. With his genius Mozart wrote the right music for *Figaro* and then, under pressure from a diva, wrote alternative arias.[3]

Miller's language here was not designed to calm the situation. Bartoli's decision to sing two arias Mozart wrote for *Le nozze di Figaro* in 1789, rather than two arias Mozart wrote for *Le nozze di Figaro* in 1786, is likened—in the first quote—to invasion by Panzer tanks; in the second he suggests that her determination not to sing "Deh vieni" in Act IV threatened to deprive sad operagoing battalions of the release they had (presumably) paid money to experience. Clearly Miller thought he had right on his side: he lined himself up, after all, with none other than W. A. Mozart, both he and the composer suffering "pressure from a diva." Many in the daily press agreed, some with piercing cries against the abuses of singers. Old battles were newly joined; this was, after all, *Mozart* in need of defense.[4]

How can one counter such certainties? To recast these offending arias as prose on the page might seem a poor substitute for Bartoli's experiment, but try we must. We can start by looking at the first and certainly less substantial of them, the one that substituted for "Venite, inginocchiatevi" in Act II. In one of the opera's many actings out of gender ambiguity, the countess and Susanna are dressing already cross-dressed

Cherubino as a woman. The substitute aria is called "Un moto di gioia," and its two-stanza text is disarmingly simple:

> Un moto di gioia
> Mi sento nel petto,
> Che annunzia diletto
> In mezzo il timor;
> Speriam che in contento
> Finisca l'affanno,
> Non sempre è tiranno
> Il fato ed amor.
>
> Di pianti di pene
> Ognor non si pasce,
> Talvolta poi nasce
> Il ben dal dolor:
> E quando si crede
> Più grave il periglio,
> Brillare si vede
> La calma maggior.

[A stirring of joy / I feel in my breast, / That foretells pleasure / In the midst of fear; / Let us hope that in happiness / Worry will end, / Fortune and love / Are not always tyrannous. / Not everyone lives by / Tears and sorrow, / Sometimes good / Is born from sorrow: / And when one thinks / The danger at its worst, / One sees shining forth / The greatest calm.]

The identity of the librettist is not certain, but it was probably Lorenzo Da Ponte, who of course wrote the libretti for both *Figaro* and *Così fan tutte*. The text is clearly intended for a strophic setting and is at best loosely related to the immediate plot situation. The aria it replaces, "Venite, inginocchiatevi," is on the other hand an "action" number, with specific references to the dramatic situation. In "Un moto di gioia" the approach is somewhat antique; the text takes a slightly distant, moralizing tone, commenting on the general situation, standing somewhat apart from the plot. No value judgments should be assumed in this distinction between the two arias: there are wonderfully effective "action" numbers in Mozart, of course; but there are also wonderfully effective "contemplative/moralizing" numbers; few of us would want to be without either.

The simplicity of the words is in some ways reflected in the simplicity of the setting (example 7 reports the first thirty-three measures of the aria): the two strophes of poetry are set to identical music, and this folk-song-like gesture is matched by uncomplicated rhythms and melodic contours. But within the strophic exterior there lies challenging detail. This is of course not at all surprising: Mozart's Teutonic brand of Italian opera had always been more crammed with orchestral and harmonic effect than was the homegrown type, a fact that had sometimes got him into trouble. Let's pause for a moment over the accompaniment to the opening vocal phrase, starting on the upbeat of m. 9, particularly coming as it does after the rudimentary (or perhaps "rustic"?) three-octave wind doublings in the orchestral introduction. Over a pedal bass, the violins double the voice and are marked to be played staccato; but the first violins are an octave higher than both the voice and the second violins, giving a kind of "halo" effect much used in late Mozartian chamber music (the string quintets in particular). The cellos and violas start by doubling the voice at the sixth, but at m. 11, coinciding with the word "sento" (I feel), they gain emphasis with a bow change and find their own melodic identity, forming a counterpoint with the voice. The richness of the resulting orchestral sonority is emphasized by the fact that the lower strings are legato against the upper strings' staccato. This combination of staccato and legato is surely tied to the words: "Un moto di gioia / Mi sento nel petto" (A stirring of joy / I feel in my breast); hesitant, mimetic of bodily movement, yet with an inner potential for the lyrical.

The most surprising aspect of the aria, though, is to come. In a piece as direct as this, we would expect the opening eight vocal bars (mm. 9–16) to be "answered" by a further eight-bar period. And so they are, at mm. 17–24; but the answer—which in tonal/rhetorical terms is clearly an "on the other hand," or a "yes, but" reply to mm. 9–16—comes not from the

EXAMPLE 7 (*continued*)

vocalist but from a choir of wind instruments, led off by the oboe and bassoon, joined by the flute. As so often in Mozart's later comic operas, this orchestral interlude gives the singer the opportunity (almost the obligation) to indulge in some stage business, to move the visible action along;[5] but it also sets up a sense of dialogue between the voice and the wind instruments, one that then continues in fragments throughout the aria. A first example of this dialogue comes at mm. 28–31, in which one limb of the descending sequence on "non sempre" is taken up, with a impudent added appoggiatura, by the wind instruments.

Two further small moments in the aria are worth highlighting. The first is the treatment of the word "tiranno" (tyrant), which occurs at mm. 32–33. The crescendo, the *fp* dynamic, the fermata over the high note (in fact the highest vocal note of the aria, and perhaps inviting some added improvisatory roulade of the part of the singer)—all this playfully gestures toward the world of serious opera, broadening the aria's frame of reference by including what we might now describe as something intertextual. The second moment comes at the very end of the aria (example 8). Up to then the melody has remained in comfortable soprano territory (g″ to d′); but at mm. 71–73 a descending scale takes the voice down suddenly into mezzo range, to low b and what we now call the "chest" voice. Incidentally, the aria, which Dr. Miller thought "twice as long" as the one it dislodges, has been recorded by Cecilia Bartoli and there lasts three minutes and eighteen seconds. The recording I have to hand of "Venite, inginocchiatevi" lasts two minutes and forty-seven seconds.[6]

There is one further point about "Un moto di gioia" that, for the moment, needs to be flagged and then put to one side. In several ways, this is music not entirely typical of Susanna in *Figaro*. The elaborate wind dialogue, the gestures to *opera seria* practice, perhaps especially that precipitate dive into the chest register at the end: all these aspects gently suggest another Mozart, above all the one we know from *Così fan tutte*. But more of that anon.

EXAMPLE 8. Wolfgang Amadeus Mozart, *Le nozze di Figaro*, "Un moto di gioia" (mm. 67–end).

At this point, I hope merely to have suggested that "Un moto di gioia" may be worth listening to and also worth thinking about: that it is, in short, worthy of the attention Mozart's mature music habitually receives. The fact is, though, that even during a period such as ours, in which the composer's slightest juvenilia can be performed in contexts of bizarre seriousness, the aria was relatively little known until Bartoli took it up. What is more, her performances brought down, on it and on her, a stream of abuse. The critic John W. Freeman, for example, again writing in *Opera News*, called it an "ersatz ditty . . . a bit of fluff that leaves a dramatic hole where 'Venite, inginocchiatevi' is supposed to be."[7] Such easy condemnations were repeated endlessly. Beside testifying to the fact that the world of *Tageskritik* can sometimes be depressingly thought-free, they are, I think, a glum reflection of the restrictive power of the work-concept in our culture. In his *Opera News* interview, Miller articulated the attitude perfectly: "With his genius Mozart wrote the right music for *Figaro*." It's a comforting thought, above all because it tells us that what we know, our reified version of the opera, is and always will be sufficient unto the day. But was Mozart's genius really so well behaved? Did he bottle it up, reserve it only for those situations in which it can now descend to us neatly packaged? in forms that can be accommodated within our present musical institutions?

The composer's evident penchant for writing substitute arias is in some ways the most apt argument against any complacency we might harbor over "our" text. The Neue Mozart Ausgabe has four volumes (more than 700 pages' worth) of such pieces, most of them rarely performed.[8] Just from the period under discussion, the second half of 1789, he wrote (in addition to the two new *Figaro* arias, instrumental trifles such as the Clarinet Quintet and, of course, *Così fan tutte*) three outstanding operatic arias for soprano and orchestra. Each of them flamboyantly violates the notion of the operatic work-concept, the idea that a late eighteenth-century composer might create "the right music" for an opera, music that must then be repeated at all subsequent revivals, no matter what the changes in performance conditions. The first, K. 578, is an insert aria Mozart wrote for a revival of Cimarosa's opera buffa *I due baroni di Rocca Azzurra* in Vienna and is remarkable both for its high tone and its experimentation with contrapuntal effects (distinctly un-Cimarosa-like, one might add, but an evident Mozartian enthusiasm of the period). The other two, K. 582 and K. 583, were inserts for another opera then on the boards in Vienna, Martín y Soler's *Il burbero di buon cuore*. The second, K. 583, "Vado, ma dove? Oh Dei!," has a slow movement, a kind of pastoral minuet, that resembles little else in Mozart. It is yet another of those elaborate dialogues between voice and a chorus of wind instruments, in this case with the richness enhanced by an almost constant juxtaposition of quarter notes in the winds and triplet accompaniment in the strings. The singer mediates between these two rhythmic worlds. To listen to this aria is to understand in a new way what a very *different* composer Mozart was becoming in the last two or three years of his life. But, to repeat the earlier question, how could he be so profligate? How could he squander such music on such an ephemeral context?

There are of course many answers to such questions. The obvious historical one is that, for Mozart, *all* operatic contexts were ephemeral; he had no certainty that his music would survive any longer than that of Cimarosa or Martín y Soler, both of whom were at the time more widely popular than he was. As discussed in chapter 1, the very idea of an "operatic repertory" had as yet little purchase. However, and partly for this reason, the late eighteenth century was conspicuously more generous than we are today in accommodating such occasional inspirations. We now feel ourselves at a great historical distance from the time when "works of genius" could be thrown off with such abandon, when some amalgam of personal and cultural faith assured everyone that more would arrive, if not tomorrow, then next season; that such works were not worth loving so jealously. We are now invaded by cultural pessimism about music and opera, perhaps about all art: a mood that makes us miserly and grasping, fearful of loss. We attach fanatical reverence to the works precisely because we doubt that what is to come will ever be as good.

In this mood of tenacious, unthinking conservation, we miss much. "Vado, ma dove?" was written for a singer called Luise Villeneuve, who was a little later to create the role of Dorabella in *Così fan tutte*; it has even been suggested that Mozart wrote the aria as a way of testing out Villeneuve's vocal skills prior to constructing her operatic character.[9] Not coincidentally, then, the piece bears unusual similarities to Dorabella's first-act aria in *Così*, "Smanie implacabili." Both are in the key of E♭, both feature prominent modal mixtures for pathos, both involve a beleaguered heroine; with tiny adjustments to the words, an adventurous soprano could substitute one for the other, thus extending the emotional range of Dorabella in *Così*, and giving us a chance to hear in a theatrical context that almost Brahmsian pastoral minuet, in some ways so suited to *Così*'s musical world. But who would dare do such a thing? Imagine the outcry. "With his genius [we would be told] Mozart wrote the right music for *Così fan tutte*."

Talk of singers, though, can lead us back to those two replacement arias for *Figaro*, the ones that so rattled Jonathan Miller's cage. As mentioned at the start, both were written because the Vienna 1789 revival of *Figaro* boasted a notable new Susanna. This was Adriana Ferrarese, who had arrived in Vienna during 1788 and had established herself as one of the most successful singers of comic opera at the Burgtheater, in spite of having been more famous previously in *opera seria*.[10] She had by all accounts a voice of impressive extension, with a powerful low register and unusual flexibility (large leaps and trills were particular specialties). Mozart would, famously, exploit these qualities when he created Fiordiligi for her in *Così fan tutte*; but, as he did with Luise Villeneuve (Ferrarese's sister both in real life and in *Così fan tutte*), he first tested the boundaries, tried her vocality on for size. The result was this pair of arias for the Vienna *Figaro*. Miller (to quote him one last time) tells us that they were written "under pressure from a diva"; a degree of coercion is sometimes also hinted at in the musicological literature but has never—

so far as I know—been convincingly documented (another case, perhaps, of an attitude to historical evidence best summed up by the Italian
motto *se non è vero, è ben trovato*).[11]

Pressure or not, we can probably see hints of Ferrarese's distinctive
vocal character in "Un moto di gioia," particularly in that unexpected,
spectacular dive below the stave reported in example 8. But it is in the
second replacement aria, the one that substitutes for Susanna's "Deh
vieni" in Act IV, that her vocal presence seems to press more obviously
on the very shape and tone of the music. We should recall the dramatic
situation in *Figaro*'s last act, then at its most complex. Susanna and the
countess have exchanged clothes in order to expose the count in his pursuit of Susanna. Susanna is left alone in the garden. Figaro is suspicious
and lurks in the obscurity. His suspicions seem confirmed when he hears
Susanna sing in eager anticipation of an amorous encounter (he cannot
see her and so does not know she is in disguise). "Deh vieni," the aria she
sings in the original version, is a character piece—a simple serenade
in §, which in general shape and tone suits the style of Susanna's music
elsewhere in the opera.

Curiously, though, the aria also makes gestures toward a more elevated style, in particular in its text, where the invocation of the sultry
night is highly poetic for a buffo character, even bordering on the
Metastasian:

> Finché non splende in ciel notturna face,
> Finché l'aria è ancor bruna, e il mondo tace.
> Qui mormora il ruscel, qui scherza l'aura.

[While the torch of night does not shine in the sky, / While the air
is still dark, and the world silent. / Here murmurs the brook, here
sports the breeze.]

What is more, Mozart clearly responded to this shift in tone by supplying an opening ritornello and relatively independent wind parts (both
musical features more likely to accompany highborn characters).[12] Why
Susanna's musical and poetic style should here bear traces of her cos-

tume, of the fact that she is disguised as the countess, is a question we shall return to; but for now it is enough merely to register the oddness. What is in no doubt is that the aria that substituted for "Deh vieni" underlines the confusion insistently from a musical point of view: it is a classic example of the two-movement *rondò*, the grandest (and longest and most aristocratic) aria type then in vogue. As is clear from the words, the sentiments—though physical and intense—are of the most general and elevated imaginable:

> Al desio di chi t'adora,
> Vieni, vola, oh mia speranza!
> Morirò, se indarno ancora
> Tu mi lasci sospirar.
> Le promesse, i giuramenti,
> Deh! rammenta, oh mio tesoro!
> E i momenti di ristoro,
> Che mi fece Amor sperar!
> Ah ch'omai più non resisto
> All'ardor che in sen m'accende.
> Chi d'amor gli affetti intende
> Compatisca il mio penar.

[To the desire of she who adores you, / Come, fly, oh my hope! / I shall die if, still in vain, / You leave me sighing. / Your promises, your oaths, / Oh, remember, my treasure! / And the moments of pleasure, / That Love made me hope for! / Ah, I can no longer resist / The ardor that enflames my breast. / Those who know the effects of love / Understand my pain.]

"Al desio" is too long to describe in great detail (lasting around six minutes, it is indeed nearly twice the length of "Deh vieni"). It follows the general pattern of rondòs of the period: split into two movements, the first slow, the second fast, both of them involving large-scale thematic repetition (hence the term *rondò*), it features elaborate vocal coloratura and, in dialogue with this, equally elaborate contributions from an unusual group of wind instruments, in this case two basset horns, two bassoons, and two French horns. Merely from the opening measures (example 9), we can see that the levels of expressive variety are extraordinary. The singer's opening triadic statement, with its expressive lean on the middle syllable of "de*si*o," is accompanied only by the wind "band"; but the disposition of parts within the winds' generally dark sonority is constantly shifting (with the character's vagrant desire?), the upper part moving from first horn to first basset horn, the bass shifting from second basset horn to bassoon and back. Then, on the *opera seria* outburst of "morirò" (m. 5), the strings appear with a rhetorical gesture; but the violins are muted, softening much of their gestural effect and instead becoming an indistinct haze of sound. The second quatrain is launched at m. 11. Those "promesse" and "giuramenti" are initially stated by the wind band in a rather stilted, banal manner: first basset horn and bassoon in parallel thirds, second basset horn chugging away in the bass.[13] But then, at m. 18, a remarkable transformation begins. With daring virtuosity, the second basset horn and first horn take on the pleading role, in an insistent counterpoint. A more serious, more seductive tone takes over; and the change has its effect on the voice, which fades momentarily into the background, perhaps sensible of the pleading instruments.

Even this much description may suggest that the aria has layers of meaning and complexity that could certainly be related to the dramatic situation for which it was intended; Mozart was certainly capable of writing routinely, even at this stage of his career, but did not do so here. It is sad to report, though, that among Mozartians, a group not famous for coolness of aesthetic judgment when their hero's music is involved, "Al desio" has had a startlingly poor press. Hardly any commentator has a good word for it. For Hermann Abert, "the piece remains an entity foreign to the opera, a concession Mozart made to a singer to whom he was not close on the artistic level."[14] For Stefan Kunze it is "sentimentalizing, in spite of its ambitious musical conception. It demonstrates that in the choice of cast [for the Vienna *Figaro*] there had been an error, and that Mozart, following the trend of the time, had to make the best of a bad job."[15] In the process of an impressively detailed analysis of Mozart's

EXAMPLE 9. Wolfgang Amadeus Mozart, *Le nozze di Figaro*, "Al desio" (mm. 1–23).

EXAMPLE 9 *(continued)*

(continued)

EXAMPLE 9 *(continued)*

EXAMPLE 9 (continued)

aria's forms, James Webster pronounces "Deh vieni" a key to Susanna's character and gets rather agitated about certain details of the aria; perhaps small wonder, then, that in a severe footnote he mentions "Al desio" only to remark on "the falseness of tone which all modern commentators find in [it]."[16] Many of the journalists at those Met performances in 1998, some of them perhaps emboldened by this overwhelmingly negative "expert" reception, were even less guarded. Anthony Tommasini, in a *New York Times* article remarkable for its intemperance of language, stated:

> The original, "Deh vieni non tardar," is utterly moving, a miracle of an aria, while "Al desio," the rondo that replaces it, is an unabashed display piece. It begins reflectively, with a simple melody, but soon evolves into a frilly, trilly, filigreed thing, like Rossini at his most bumptious.[17]

For most of these commentators, whether musicological or journalistic, the very existence of what they pronounce poor music—by the mature Mozart—is *so* extraordinary, *so* against nature, that it immediately solicits a narrative explanation; there needs, and that urgently, to be a villain in the tale. And of course, as Abert and Kunze both made plain, a stock operatic figure stands ready at hand, in the person of the diva Ferrarese. The fact that the composer made two disparaging remarks about her in his letters adds further welcome ammunition. Quoted almost invariably is a comment to his wife, Constanze, about "Un moto di gioia": "The arietta, which I've composed for Madame Ferrarese, ought, I think, to please, if she is capable of singing it in an artless manner, which I very much doubt."[18] The fact that the latter stages of "Al desio" involve, as do all rondòs, a great deal of florid singing is yet further proof: never trust a trilling soprano (and this whether she steps out of history or interrupts the Met at their Mozartian prayer—the similarity between musicological treatments of Ferrarese and journalistic treatments of Bartoli is gloomily obvious). More than this, and to tie a pink ribbon around the stereotype, there's the rou-

tinely repeated assertion that Ferrarese was at the time Lorenzo Da
Ponte's mistress (he boasts of it in his memoirs, as he does of the fact
that, some years after their falling out, he managed to damage her career
by making negative remarks about her in high places).[19]

This mighty chorus of disapproval is unlikely to be stilled, supported
as it is by such an orchestra of easy assumptions, of attitudes that would
hardly be tolerated if stated baldly, but that are none the less handy when
a "work" needs protection. Let me list a few of the more obvious: that
first versions are likely to be better than revisions when the latter are
known to have been stimulated by practical necessity rather than "artistic" reasons (as if one can ever neatly distinguish between the two); that
when performers are suspected of having influence over composers, it is
likely to be unwelcome and can be assumed to have taken place under
duress; that elaborate vocal virtuosity is to be regarded with suspicion,
perhaps especially when the purveyor of such heady delights is female;
that long arias in which the stage action is frozen are less "operatic" or
less "dramatic" than those that feature dialogue and/or plenty of stage
movement. And so on and on. Indeed, writers have been so sure they
want to keep "Al desio" out of *Figaro* that (to my knowledge) no one has
felt obliged to look at it with a view to what it might create within the
opera, what new contexts might emerge from its inclusion. This is a pity,
because such contexts can, I think, potentially be important for the way
we think about the ending of Mozart's opera.

Let me start with a point about "Al desio" so obvious that it comes as
a surprise to find no mention of it in the Mozart literature: while the aria
is clearly very different in proportion, form, and gesture from "Deh
vieni," there exist important similarities between them. They are in the
same key (a point those arguing for elaborate tonal plans in the opera
always remark on with relieved approval), and of course they share the
same preceding recitative, "Giunse alfin il momento." More than this,
though, they have in many places a distinctly similar melodic stamp, in
particular a tendency for simple diatonic language and arpeggiated
cadential figures. These similarities might encourage us to think of the

arias as (at least potentially) part of the same dramatic project: they can both, for example, be thought tied to a distinctive nocturnal-pastoral ambience. But it is also true that they articulate that ambience in sharply different ways: as already mentioned, "Deh vieni" evokes the night through its rich, "high-toned" poetic imagery and simple accompaniment; "Al desio," in contrast, makes the nocturnal atmosphere musically manifest in quite other fashion, those basset horns in particular suggesting that here the night is more tenebrous, the moon more veiled.

This is important because it involves a famous crux in *Figaro*, one on which the substitution of "Al desio" has a potentially important effect. Recall the scene: Susanna and the countess have exchanged clothes; Susanna is now on her own, overheard but unseen by Figaro; she sings the aria as part of a performance—to trick Figaro into thinking that she is eager for a liaison with the count. So, although dressed as another, she should be singing in "her own" voice. But not really "her own," as the sentiments she articulates are feigned (a liaison with the count is, of course, what she has spent the entire opera avoiding). Some of this ambiguity can be heard in "Deh vieni," which has musical and poetic elements that are markedly "elevated" for Susanna. The aria nevertheless remains—as music, and in the voice it commands—broadly in the *buffo* world proper to her character. Indeed, it has been suggested, by James Webster most enthusiastically, that Susanna "reveals her true self" during the course of the aria, specifically with those "liquid, undulating violin motifs" near the end.[20] In this context, "Al desio" is much more obviously a musical *travestimento*. There are now mere traces of *buffo* character; in general Susanna sings with tones that are unambiguously elevated.

I would be the first to agree that "Deh vieni," with its artful simplicity, is an astonishing Mozartian moment; but I would nevertheless question whether its solution is so obviously better, so *permanently* better, than that of "Al desio." The libretto's establishment of a kinship, an emotional equality even, between Susanna and the countess, something made iconic when they exchange clothes in the final act, is after all one of the central issues of the drama. What is more, we also know that, probably for practical reasons that emerged during rehearsal, Mozart changed his mind about the vocal disposition of his two sopranos, particularly about who should take the upper part in ensembles.[21] In other words, these two characters continually weave in and out of each other's vocal personality: as musical presences, they have already been confounded. At an early stage, Mozart even sketched a rondò for the first Susanna, Nancy Storace—and to judge by the highly strenuous two-tempo concert aria he wrote for her in 1786, she would have been fully up to the task.[22] What is more, Storace was well known for her ability to imitate others, and, famously, just a little after "Al desio" Susanna indeed disguises her voice, trying to fool Figaro into thinking she is the countess.[23] In all this concatenation of confused identities, it would be a brave critic who insisted, insisted so rigidly and with so little room for equivocation, that a particular vocal identity is *necessary* for Susanna in her nocturnal aria, at this moment alone. But when scholars believe that Mozart's original intentions are marching behind them, many become brave.

There is, though, another confusion of voices caused by "Al desio," one that could take us through a long line of rondòs and through some of Mozart's most imposing vocal music, most obviously those for Donna Anna in *Don Giovanni*, for Fiordiligi in *Così fan tutte*, and for Sesto in *La clemenza di Tito*. If we believe John Rice, we can witness Mozart in this series of pieces engaged in a fascinating emulative tussle with Antonio Salieri.[24] But of course the principal connection in this case is to the part that Adriana Ferrarese would soon create, to Fiordiligi in *Così*, an opera with which—as I mentioned earlier—Mozart was in all likelihood already engaged at the time he was writing "Al desio." Fiordiligi's great rondò in Act II of *Così*, "Per pietà, ben mio, perdona," has much in common with "Al desio," the latter seeming almost like a trial run for the former. Some of these similarities are of course generic, reflecting the formal conventions of the rondò: the two-tempo form, the prominent use of wind instruments, the florid writing in the second section. But others are more personal, almost certainly inspired by placing the same singer in dramatic situations that have much in common. A glance at the verses of "Per pietà" will make the similarities plain:

> Per pietà, ben mio, perdona
> All'error d'un'alma amante;
> Fra quest'ombre e queste piante
> Sempre ascoso, o Dio, sarà.
> Svenerà quest'empia voglia
> L'ardir mio, la mia costanza,
> Perderà la rimembranza
> Che vergogna e orror mi fa.
> A chi mai mancò di fede
> Questo vano ingrato cor!
> Si dovea miglior mercede
> Caro bene, al tuo candor!

[Have pity, my love, forgive / The fault of a loving soul; / Among these shadowy groves / It will, oh God, always be hidden. / My courage, my passion, / Will empty my veins of this wicked desire, / Will drive out the memory / Which gives me shame and horror. / Whom did it betray, / This worthless, empty heart! / You deserved a better reward / My beloved, for your sincerity!]

Both "Al desio" and "Per pietà" take place in a garden, a place that provides shadows and seclusion and thus allows secret thoughts to emerge, thoughts of illicit desire, of amorous feelings that need to be hidden from the world. In both cases this sense of the thing that must remain hidden is partly evoked by the voice, which makes prominent show of the lower register in quiet contexts. Most obviously, though, it emerges in the shared use of the solo horn, a horn that betrays its usual orchestral nature by duetting with the soloist, by invading the realm of the lyrical. There is probably a gesture here to the old pun, the horn, the *corno*, signifying the cuckold's horns, as it will so violently in Figaro's jealousy aria "Aprite un po' quegl'occhi," the aria that follows immediately on "Al desio" in the fourth act of *Figaro*. In these two rondòs for Ferrarese, though, the horns are anything but brazen and mocking.

Their proximity to, their merging with, vocal expression make us aware, with an economy of which music is uniquely capable, of a famous ambiguity at the heart of *Così fan tutte:* of the fact that "illicit" emotions, ones that flourish in the shadows, are not always neatly separated from others, more socially acceptable; that the cuckold's horn can sometimes bring forth sounds of painful beauty.

What can we gain from pondering these similarities? Just as those gypsies danced into Verdi's *La traviata,* so a breath of *Così fan tutte* has strayed into the last act of *Figaro,* ushered in by the distinctive voice of Adriana Ferrarese. Fiordiligi, Mozart's most ambivalent character, is now part of *Figaro,* leaving her mark on a Susanna dressed as the countess, changing the landscape. Inserting "Al desio" into *Figaro,* in other words, gives us a glimpse of another Mozartian operatic world, not just in the technical sense (shared by "Un moto di gioia") of introducing a richness of wind writing that is typical of *Così* but rare in *Figaro,* but also, more important, one in which the business of sexual jealousy is approached very differently, where the denouement that sets everything "right" carries less weight. The extent to which the *Figaro* landscape changes when it embraces "Al desio" will of course depend on performers' choices. But the possibilities are enticing. The presence of the aria might, for example, encourage Susanna to be a little more taken by the count than either the libretto or her protestations allow: to use Carolyn Abbate's now-famous term, "voice Count" is, after all, disturbingly likeable. What then haunts "Al desio" is the forbidden possibility—of female attraction to the wrong, or subversive, or dramatically illogical object of desire.

In this sense, far from dispersing the tension of that moment in the garden, "Al desio" meaningfully darkens *Figaro.* But there is more. Its presence, its difference, its moment of excess, may cause us to reassess the terms of the vocal contracts we have wrapped around this and other Mozart operas. The countess, Susanna, Fiordiligi: we tend to understand these characters, make them "ours," in part by means of a rigid classification of vocal types. Mozart, though, was writing for real voices, for individual women and men. Rhetorically, we often forget this:

Mozart wrote music, not words, not characters, not libretto. The influence of a singular voice and individual is not a matter of reproach, but something positive for the formation of *his* work (music), a something perhaps more positive than we want to imagine. To put this one last way, Adriana Ferrarese's "Al desio" can usefully confuse us, make us aware that Susanna does not have to remain locked in one particular vocal mold. She can, in this fourth act of *Le nozze di Figaro*, vocally become the countess, assume more forcefully a position we thought could not be hers. And she can, by means of a horn solo and certain low notes, vocally become Fiordiligi, bringing with her an ambiguity that can add further layers of complexity to Mozart's ever-mutable opera.

FOUR

In Search of Verdi

My main port of call in this chapter is Verdi's *Falstaff*, and that choice, together with the title and several other matters, has brought with it an obligation: I find myself constrained to trail a hand in the shark-infested waters that surround themes such as modernity and late style, not least as these dark topics have been presented to a mostly bewildered world by Theodor W. Adorno.[1] Before embarkation a confession had better be made. I don't much like Adorno; or, better, I dislike what Adorno has come to stand for in the musicological community; and my attitude, which has been unbending for about twenty years, hardly changed when, quite recently, I got around to reading closely some of his copious and dense writings on music. My lame, inadequate excuse for ignoring him had always been that my central interests are with Italian music, while Adorno's musical world was almost exclusively and unapologetically peopled by Austro-German composers; his book *In Search of Wagner*, for example (which has frequent references to august Wagnerian predecessors such as Mozart and Beethoven, and august followers, such as Schoenberg and Berg), has, so far as I've been able to find, just one reference to the Italian operatic tradition from which Wagner learned so much, and it's a fairly contemptuous aside about Rossini.[2] True, Adorno is also pretty tough on Wagner. But at least he wrote a book to ventilate his attitude. The chances of our finding in his ever-expanding *Nachlaß* an unknown manuscript called *In Search of Verdi* seem remote.

But there is another aspect to my Adornophobia. His writings are of course famously difficult, in part because famously contradictory; the suspicion arises that this complexity of discourse has itself been a siren song for disciples. What is more, his impressive density of utterance has had the effect of making much commentary on him merely explanatory; the perceived need for exegesis has often crowded out hermeneutic activity. Discussing what Adorno might have intended has, in other words, sometimes too readily stood in for discussing what he actually said, for critically engaging with his ideas. So much so that to treat him as one would most other writers on music—to measure his propositions against the musical evidence he cites, for example—risks seeming rather prosaic, if not downright dogged and literal.[3] However, I must in this chapter both begin and end by taking that risk, because although I want primarily to address a rather curious moment in *Falstaff*, it serves my purpose to depart on the journey with a passage from *In Search of Wagner* under my arm.

My chosen passage sees Adorno discussing Wagner's compositional habits, and it can stand as a typical example of what Peter J. Martin has recently called Adorno's "grand narrative" of the function of music in the last few hundred years of Western culture, a narrative in which (to quote Martin) "the emergence and decay of tonality is taken as a symbolic representation of the rise and fall of the ideology of bourgeois individualism."[4] The passage attempts to develop an idea Adorno had stated a few sentences before, namely that "the working methods of major composers have always contained elements of technical rationalization." This by no means limpid statement is then clarified somewhat. Adorno outlines Wagner's compositional methods, what he calls the "objectifying" of a penciled draft of unorchestrated musical material by means of a parallel and near contemporary process of orchestral sketching. This he sees as

> preventing the sound . . . from achieving independence. . . . The
> short interval between the two stages makes it possible to retain a

grasp of the orchestral colour that had been conceived in the original act of composition. This gives some indication of the ingenuity with which Wagner organized the division of labor. It encompasses all the layers of his composition and makes possible that interlocking of its elements, which closes all gaps and creates the impression of absolute cohesion and immediacy. The magical effect is inseparable from the same rational process of production that it attempts to exorcize.

Wagner's division of labor is that of an individual. This sets limits to it, which is perhaps why it has to be so strenuously denied.[5]

Adorno's pronouncement here is, as I said, typical of at least one of his tactics. A small, rather technical feature (in this case a detail about Wagner's compositional process) suddenly finds itself dragooned into radical interpretive service, this by force of assertion rather than by means of argument, with the whole package then neatly closed off with the flourish of a paradox. If we cast the passage loose from its rhetorical context for a moment, questions come flooding in. What, for example, does it mean to say that orchestration "prevent[s] the sound . . . from achieving independence"? How can "sound" have agency in this sense? Reading between others of his lines, one can guess that the gesture is to an idea that somewhere (on the page?) sound can be stripped of timbre, made pure form or pure relationship between pitches; but is operatic sound ever thus? Such equivocation leads to another question: how does the employment of orchestral detail "[encompass] all the layers of his composition" and "[close] all gaps and [create] the impression of absolute cohesion and immediacy"? No explanation is offered for these bold equations and—this is my principal objection—the resulting absence is covered over by hectoring, inflationary words such as "prevent," "all," and "absolute cohesion."

So my dislike (or, better, distrust) of Adorno remains, I'm afraid. But I will nevertheless admit that I now find his writings curiously stimulating, principally because his reckless leaps from small musical detail into sweeping worldview are bold enough, passionate enough, even, to encourage me to think again about where musical meaning might most convincingly be located in the larger picture. For example, even though I find the critical approach he essays in that passage about Wagner—of seeing compositional method as in some way revealing "inner meaning"—is in its local context preposterous, it can all the same have interesting ramifications for the contemplation of *Falstaff*, in particular for the part of it I want to address here. But to go further along that route, I need some historical detail, some musicological grounding in late Verdi.

One of the noticeable aspects of Verdi's late compositional practice is that there emerged important discontinuities, both with his previous methods and, arguably, within the works themselves. His lifelong practice had been to move chronologically through various layers of composition: I explained something about these layers in chapter 2, which involved the sketches for *La traviata:* first Verdi sketched out individual numbers (the important set pieces) in short score (usually just a melody and bass); then he fashioned a continuity draft of the entire opera in the same format; then came a skeleton score (including all the important vocal lines and some instrumental lines), entered into the autograph score; and only after all that was completed, typically at a very late stage, often during rehearsals with the singers in the theater where the premiere was to take place, did he add the orchestration.[6] In this sense, perhaps, Verdi might have been approved of by Adorno: his compositional method, which typically isolated the various creative phases, arguably allowed room for the "sound" to achieve "independence." Whether we'd like to argue that this is what happened is, of course, quite another matter. But it's obvious that "orchestral thought" in the sense implied by Adorno, a sense typically used in connection with "advanced" twentieth-century music, rarely occurs in Verdi, even late Verdi. This "lifelong compositional practice" was not unvarying—card-carrying Verdians will all be able to think of exceptions—but it was nevertheless the standard operating procedure. Even as late as the revisions to *Simon Boccanegra* in the early 1880s, Verdi told his librettist Arrigo Boito that "I will begin working on the first number of the first act, if for no other reason than to put myself *dans le mouvement* before arriving at the finale."[7] Here, and elsewhere, Verdi's need to be—compositionally, creatively—*dans le mouvement* of an opera as he worked on it seemed important, and we can readily understand why.

But the last two operas are different. Alterations to his lifelong compositional pattern can be found, albeit in a minor way, during the creation of *Otello* (again in the 1880s). After writing a continuity draft in largely chronological fashion, Verdi then immediately set about entering the skeleton score of and then orchestrating the final act, as he said "to finish completely, including the orchestration, in order to seal it shut and not speak of it any more."[8] With *Falstaff*, though, the discontinuities become much more striking.[9] So far as we can tell, the orchestration of several sections was completed before other sections were even in draft, a situation unprecedented elsewhere in his career. We might immediately want to talk, in classic late-style terms, of a "fragmentation" of the discourse, something Adorno famously advanced in relation to both Beethoven and Wagner;[10] but there may also be more prosaic reasons (albeit ones that could co-exist with the fragmentation hypothesis), an obvious one being that Verdi at his advanced age feared he might forget details of the orchestration if he didn't write them down (or, in his revealing words, "seal them shut").

In the case of *Falstaff* there is also a central narrative redundancy embedded in this changed practice: the problem of what to do with the third act, something identified by Boito (again his librettist) very early in the genesis of the opera. As Boito saw it—and Verdi agreed—the opera was in a certain important sense over after the antics of Act II, scene 2. The first two acts are scenically and musically symmetrical (their first scenes are in the Garter Inn; their second scenes in Ford's house), and during the course of these four scenes Falstaff's humiliation is magnificently accomplished, the climax coming at the end of Act II when he is ceremoniously tipped into the Thames along with a basketful of stinking clothes. Here is how Boito formulated the problem of what might come next:

In comedy there's a moment when the audience says *"It's finished,"* but when on stage the action has to continue. A knot can't be unraveled without being loosened first, and when it's loose, the solution can be foreseen and the interest is gone before the knot is. Comedy unravels the knot; tragedy breaks or severs it. So the third act of *Falstaff* is of course the coldest.[11]

Their solution in Act III, scene 2 (the last in the opera), was, daringly, to concoct a "fantastic" episode in Windsor Great Park, a scene whose atmosphere in many respects barely recalls the rest of the opera. But what to do about Act III, scene 1? Verdi and Boito had first imagined a grand duet for the young lovers Fenton and Nannetta, but when (Boito's idea) their music got fragmented, their exchanges sprinkled through the rest of the score, there seemed little to put in its place: a repetition of the protagonist's interview with Mistress Quickly, to make a new assignation in Windsor Great Park (complete with prominent leitmotivic recollections of the earlier scene), seemed all that was necessary, and of course this repetition merely emphasized the fact that the same action sequence (Falstaff is again to be lured by Mistress Quickly, then trapped and humiliated) is being, well, repeated.

Perhaps the presence of this narrative void is partly why Verdi left Act III, scene 1, until last. Reaching the end of Act II, scene 2, in skeleton score, he skipped to Act III, scene 2, the Windsor Great Park finale. Even more surprising, when he came to the end of the opera, he then immediately set about orchestrating the early parts more fully, this time admitting explicitly that he was afraid of forgetting some passages and instrumental textures.[12] And he kept going right through to the end of the opera, again jumping over Act III, scene 1. It seems, then, that most of the rest (if not all) of *Falstaff* was fully orchestrated before Verdi settled down to this troublesome first scene of Act III. Recall here what Verdi said about Act IV of *Otello*. He orchestrated it "to finish completely, including the orchestration, in order to seal it shut and not speak of it any more." At this stage in *Falstaff* Verdi had, then, orchestrated himself into a corner: he found himself with a work that was finished but also unfinished, sealed but unsealed. Act III, scene 1, remained a phantom open to the void.[13]

I belabor this chronology because the scene that eventually emerged seems to me one of the most extraordinary in all Verdi. It is full of disjointed reminiscences of earlier scenes, but (much more radically) it also has musical *anticipations* of the scene in Windsor Great Park that follows (particularly of its highly original sound world), anticipations that I assume were made possible because the latter scene already existed as music in an almost finished form. So far as I know, this is the only time—formal preludes apart—in which Verdi, in a finished score, anticipated a sound world still to come in this way; where hints are given of a distinctive sonorous atmosphere that will emerge fully only later in the score.[14] Indeed, it is difficult to think of circumstances in which such anticipations might usually function in Verdi's determinedly "present" dramatic world; so much so that we might immediately think of the sense of rupture that is one side of the discourse on aging and its creative products.

A brief description of the progress of the scene will be useful here. We are outside the Garter Inn, at sunset. Falstaff is deeply dejected after his enforced swim in the Thames, but he revives when presented with a large tankard of *vin caldo* (mulled wine). He is interrupted by Quickly; excuses are made, and another assignation, this time at midnight in Windsor Great Park, is fixed. Quickly leads Falstaff into the inn, hinting darkly at the supernatural forces at work in the park. The conspirators (who have been hidden observers of the scene) now emerge, and they also invoke the mysteries and terror of the place. But they shake them off and plan for the masquerade to come. The scene ends in a passage of remarkable dissolution. The characters gradually leave the stage in groups, calling to each other as darkness descends. In the closing moments, the stage empty and almost completely dark, the orchestra itself seems to float upward and disappear.

It would be tempting to dwell on the mysteries, the evocation of terror that (even in this most knowing of operas) not a single character, nor the librettist, nor the composer—cynical and practical though they may be—is willing to dismiss or resolve as mere comic anxiety. But there is a further node in this scene, again having to do with *how* Verdi went about the business of composition. The final pages gave him some trouble. As the first run of performances at La Scala, Milan, was coming to an end, and the first vocal score was already on sale, he decided to revise them radically, jettisoning one reminiscence from earlier in the scene (Alice's $\frac{3}{4}$ "Fandonie che ai bamboli"), or rather refashioning its dominating musical gesture in an entirely different rhythmic context (the $\frac{4}{4}$ "march" figure that follows Alice's "Provvedi le lanterne"), and also extending the appearance of a further reminiscence (Alice's "Avrò con me dei putti").[15] Verdi's comments to his publisher about the revision are interesting:

> I never liked that sort of mazurka that ends the first part of Act III . . . and then there was right there under one's eyes a motive ("Avrò con me dei putti") that, played and modulated well, would have been more effective; and it was also appropriate and more musical.[16]

The revisions are even more harmonically adventurous than the original, and it seems likely that the change from $\frac{3}{4}$ reminiscence to $\frac{4}{4}$ reminiscence was to some extent dictated by this desire to increase the passage's chromatic density (hence Verdi's reference to the new motive, "played and modulated well"): the $\frac{4}{4}$ tune invites modulatory meandering, while the "mazurka" has such activity somewhat heavy-handedly cast upon it. But the most surprising aspect of the revisions is the sense it gives of music composed of small, developmental fragments that could be endlessly juggled. Passages common to both versions emerge in the midst of otherwise completely changed contexts; a quotation that launched the first version and was then forgotten is now used (with its original harmony) to close off the revision. Such permutations could, one senses, have continued; that they end where they did may—interestingly from an interpretative point of view—be thought compositional accident, or exhaustion, or boredom, or practical necessity.

Nowhere, though, is the sense of bricolage in this scene more evident than in its opening, which after a dynamic orchestral introduction (itself a quotation from the preceding scene and dominated by a hectic orchestral staccato) proceeds to a monologue for Falstaff whose near-atonality is matched by a startling level of motivic disjunction, even by the standards of the opera as a whole. At about the midpoint comes the lowest moment in Falstaff's spirits, a point stressed by the near breakdown of the poetic structure—uncanny white spaces and dashes, with only the end rhymes holding the fragmentary phrases together:

Mondo reo.—Non c'è più virtù—Tutto declina.
Va, vecchio John, va, va per la tua via; cammina
Finchè tu muoia.—Allor scomparirà la vera
Virilità dal mondo.
Che giornataccia nera.
M'aiuti il ciel!—Impinguo troppo.—Ho dei peli grigi.

> (*ritorna l'Oste portando su d'un vassoio un gran bicchiere di vino caldo.—Mette il bicchiere sulla panca e rientra nell'osteria*)

Versiamo un po' di vino nell'acqua del Tamigi.

> (*beve sorseggiando ed assaporando. Si sbottonà il panciotto, si sdraia, ribeve a sorsate, rianimandosi poco a poco*)

[Wicked world. There is no virtue left. Everything in decline. / Go, old Jack, go, go thy ways; walk / Until you die. / Then true manhood / Will disappear from the world. What a black, horrible day. / Heaven help me! I'm getting too fat. My hair is going gray. / (*the innkeeper returns, carrying on a tray a large tankard of mulled wine. He puts the tankard on the bench and goes back into the inn.*) / Let's pour a little wine into the Thames water. / (*he drinks, sipping and savoring. He unbuttons his waistcoat, stretches out, drinks again in large gulps, gradually recovering his spirits*)]

The music of this central episode appears as example 10. A growling, rhythmically ambiguous unison motive in the low winds and brass punctuates Falstaff's gloomy ruminations. He tries to cheer himself with a musical reminiscence of his triumphant ditty in Act II, scene 1, "Va, vecchio John," but the "virilità," the world's manhood, has vanished, and the theme is now in a gloomy minor mode. After a brief reprise of the prelude, a second mysterious orchestral unison motive appears (marked on the fourth page of example 10 with boxes). "Che giornataccia nera" (What a black, horrible day) sings Falstaff; "M'aiuti il ciel!—Impinguo troppo.—Ho dei peli grigi" (Heaven help me! I'm getting too fat. My hair is going gray). This is the dark center of the monologue: to all intents and purposes it is without tonality; the voice is dislocated even from the reiterated motive in the bass; for a brief moment—the only such moment in the opera—Falstaff stares at himself with bleak honesty, perhaps knowing that soon he will be babbling of green fields and fumbling with the sheets of his final bed.

To punctuate these musings, a masked and muffled presence loiters in those boxes in example 10, one that several commentators have alluded to. This strange chromatic shape might seem to emerge naturally from its musical surroundings: its opening minor third encapsulates the meager span of the previous two bars of recollection, while the minor-sixth span of the entire motive (c♯–a) repeats at pitch the minor sixth of the violin figure a few bars before (over the words "cammina finchè tu muoia. Allor"). But the motive's presence is nevertheless unsettling, exuding undoubted menace but also extending charm of an enigmatic kind.[17] What is more, though, these few notes can tread a motivic path from *Falstaff* to the opera that challenges it as the most famous late opera of the fin de siècle. I'm referring of course to Wagner's *Parsifal*, and to the boxed music's similarity to (in effect identity with) a theme traditionally called the "Verführungs" motive and prominent (among many other places) in the opening of Wagner's second act, which takes place in Klingsor's magic garden. In example 11 the Wagnerian figure at the *Falstaff* transposition is itself boxed; and even from this brief context one can see that this particular sounding of the theme comes at a musically important moment—at the start of a new dynamic cycle, and one in which the developmental contour of the theme changes decisively.[18] *Parsifal* had first been performed at Bayreuth in 1882, some eleven years before *Falstaff*, and although in accordance with Wagner's wishes it had not by 1893 been publicly staged, vocal scores of the opera were available, and Verdi certainly owned a copy.[19]

EXAMPLE 10. Giuseppe Verdi, *Falstaff*, Act III, scene 1.

(continued)

EXAMPLE 10 *(continued)*

cam-mi - na fin-chè tu muo - ia.   Al - lor_____ scom-pa - ri-

EXAMPLE 10 *(continued)*

(continued)

EXAMPLE 10 *(continued)*

F. Che gior-na-tac-cia ne-ra. M'a - iu - ti il

ciel! Im-pin-guo trop-po. Ho dei pe - li gri-gi.

EXAMPLE 10 *(continued)*

(continued)

EXAMPLE 10 *(continued)*

Not surprisingly, connections between the two "last works" were soon made. The French journalist Jules Huret, for example, reported on the Paris premiere of *Falstaff* in 1894, noting the tremendous pre-performance excitement aroused by Verdi's presence and stating that it was "as if Wagner himself were returning to conduct *Parsifal*."[20] Perhaps even more revealing is an interview Verdi may have given in 1890, already at work on *Falstaff*, to another journalist, Étienne Destranges (rather charmingly referred to by Boito as "a Frenchman, but one of the nice ones"). I say "may have given" because Verdi later complained that Destranges had grossly distorted their conversation. After encouraging Verdi to disparage several of the most prominent French composers of the day (Saint-Saëns, for example, is described as "mentally ill"), the interviewer guides him into deeper waters: "At one moment I steered [the conversation] towards Wagner. I was curious to know what Verdi thought about the composer of *Parsifal*. The aged maestro replied in just two words: 'Ah, him!'"[21]

EXAMPLE II. Richard Wagner, *Parsifal*, Act II, scene I.

There is, I think, the shard of another reference to the start of Act II of *Parsifal* in this opening scene of Act III; but in at least one respect it is very different from the "Verführungs" motive moment, as it presents a reassuringly ironic reversal of the Wagnerian model. Both Verdi's orchestral prelude to the scene (the hectic staccato) and Wagner's prelude to Act II of *Parsifal* are obsessively concerned with repeated sixteenth-note patterns in the strings, but with the crucial difference that Verdi's is staccato and mostly diatonic, while Wagner's is legato and mostly chromatic. What is more, the brilliant diatonic gesture and first violin descent that precedes Falstaff's first words in the entire monologue (and immediately follows the appearance of that much-needed injection of *vin caldo* at the end of example 10) contrasts with the tortured, *Tristan*esque, half-diminished chord and similar first violin descent that ushers in Klingsor's famous opening words, "Die Zeit ist da" (again, Verdi's gesture is a kind of diatonic mirror image of Wagner's).

It is immediately tempting (I have succumbed in previous publications)[22] to juxtapose intertextual moments such as this with certain Verdi letters of the period. He comments to Boito in July 1891, for example, on Bruneau's unashamedly Wagner-influenced opera *Le rêve*, in which he complained that "there is throughout the opera a constant use of slurred notes, with an effect that must be quite monotonous. Further, a frightful abuse of dissonances that make you want to shout, like Falstaff, for the 'brief respite' of a perfect triad!"[23] In this context the ironic reversals just mentioned—the aggressive staccati of the Verdi's orchestral opening vs. Wagner's legato, that brazen perfect triad that ushers in Falstaff's first words vs. Wagner's half-diminished chord to usher in Klingsor—could be thought richly resonant. There is also the fact that, in one of his few epistolary comments about this first scene of Act III, Verdi made specific reference to the fact that the ending of the scene (that disappearing orchestra mentioned earlier) carried for him an ironic reference to Wagner:

> Here what is needed is . . . I have to say a *motive*, which diminishes, fading into pianissimo, perhaps with a solo violin in the catwalks above the stage. Why not? If now they put orchestras in the cellar,

why couldn't we put a violin in the attic? . . . If I were a prophet my apostles would say . . . *Oh what a sublime idea! . . . Ha ha ha ha!* What a beautiful world this is!![24]

Verdi spells out here what looks like a mechanical reversal of Wagnerian practice of precisely the kind we see in the prelude to Act III cited above. Wagner has an orchestra buried under the stage, I'll have one in the catwalks *above* the stage; his disciples abuse dissonances, I'll celebrate perfect triads; they indulge in constant slurs, I'll indulge in constant staccati.

But Verdi's attitude to Wagner was of course more complex than this juxtaposition suggests. Particularly when confronted with the polemics flying back and forth at the time, it is difficult—even after more than a century—to arrive at a balanced view; but two moments are worth recollecting. The first is way back in the early 1870s, around the time of *Aida.* Writing to his publisher, Giulio Ricordi, Verdi recommends performance conditions for his new opera:

get rid of those stage boxes, taking the curtain right to the footlights; and also make *the orchestra invisible.* This idea isn't mine, it's Wagner's: and it's excellent. It seems impossible that in this day and age people tolerate seeing tired evening dress and white ties mixed up with, for example, Egyptian, Assyrian or Druidic costumes; and, what is more, seeing the massed ranks of the orchestra, *which is part of the fictional world,* almost in the middle of the stalls, amongst the whistlers or the applauders.[25]

We can learn from this letter that, at least in one rather basic sense, Verdi saw both himself and Wagner as equally "avant-garde" in their desire to concentrate and intensify the effect of the operatic event—through technological and other means ensuring that spectators immerse themselves (perhaps surrender themselves) ever more completely to the "fictional world."

My second moment occurs in another famous Verdi letter, again to Giulio Ricordi. It is dated 14 February 1883, the day after Wagner's death in Venice:

> Triste Triste Triste!
> Vagner è morto!
> Leggendone jeri il dispaccio ne fui, sto per dire, atterrito. Non discutiamo.—È una grande individualità che sparisce! Un nome che lascia un'impronta potentissima nella Storia dell'Arte![26]

> Sad Sad Sad!
> Wagner is dead!
> Reading the news yesterday, I was, I don't know, struck with terror. There can be no argument.—A great personality has disappeared! A name that has left a most powerful mark on the history of art!

This letter, on the surface quite simple, is in several ways rather odd. Its melodramatic opening ("Triste Triste Triste! Vagner è morto!") could be the beginning of a grand lamenting aria, but its uncertain searching for words suggests genuine involvement mixed perhaps with genuine confusion (Verdi is *atterrito*, struck with terror rather than the conventional "regret" or "sorrow"). But the most significant moment is surely at the close. The handwritten original of this letter shows us that Verdi first wrote: "has left a powerful *(potente)* mark," but then he crossed through *potente* with a double stroke of the pen and wrote over the top *potentissima*. Just how important *was* Wagner? Verdi, quite possibly aware that this letter was likely to survive him, itself become part of the "history of art," is revealingly indecisive.

As the 1880s rolled on, and as Wagner*ism* took hold ever more powerfully, Verdi's attitude hardened. Time and again he inveighed against the manner in which the Wagnerian style was now a pan-European phenomenon and had even turned the heads of young Italian composers. A typical jeremiad, from the late 1880s:

> Our young Italian composers are not good patriots. If the Germans, starting out with Bach, have arrived at Wagner, they are acting like good Germans, and that's fine. But we descendants of Palestrina, if we imitate Wagner, we commit a musical sin, and our labors are useless, even damaging.[27]

And there was plenty more where that came from. During the last thirty years of his life, Verdi's letters and public pronouncements seem constantly to lament the unfortunate influence of Wagnerism on young Italians, the dangers of harmonic and orchestral complexity for its own sake, in particular the errors of composers who he considered had been lured onto the rocks by imitating the "symphonic" style. Instead they should return to their national roots, learn counterpoint, revere Palestrina and the great choral traditions of Italy's musical past.[28]

However, such comforting links between Verdi's written words and his final opera should not be the end of the story; Falstaff's monologue at the start of Act III, scene 1 (not to mention the entire scene, still less the entirety of *Falstaff*), cannot be enclosed within such simple binaries. For one thing, and as Linda Hutcheon and others have pointed out, parody in the nineteenth century is rarely just a matter of simple mechanical reversal.[29] And as if gently to remind us of these equivocations, at the center of the monologue there is that sudden incursion of the foreign, the alien work. That quotation from *Parsifal* at "Che giornataccia nera" is a reference so far from ironic, appearing as it does at the point of a character's ruthless self-examination, at the moment of bleak honesty, that it invokes anything but distance from the object so magically conjured up.

For me, this moment in the score is of significance precisely because of its detachment from its surroundings. It is an isolated, unrepeated fragment in a score full of internal repetitions and cross-references. It is embedded in a scene that was in some basic narrative sense unnecessary and for this reason became dislocated in the compositional chronology. Recall what Adorno said of *Parsifal*: the process of orchestral sketching "encompasses all the layers of his composition and makes possible that interlocking of its elements, which closes all gaps and creates the impression of absolute cohesion and immediacy." Here, conversely, we have a *breaking loose* from the layers of composition, something that makes possible a *dislocation* of elements, that *opens* gaps and *dissolves* the impression of absolute cohesion and immediacy. We are, in other words, on the threshold of modernity, of our modernity: Falstaff, and with him Verdi, seem to gaze toward a future that will inevitably, and soon, be without them; and their gaze is bleak and honest.

I'm on the edge of large claims here, claims that others have made with greater force and in greater detail. Albeit via a different route, I'm in complete agreement with a fresh trend in thinking about *Falstaff*, one that wishes to place the opera more firmly within its period of composition.[30] Since those very first, hagiographically uncomprehending reviews of the opera, the twentieth century's tendency has always been to close the work off, casting it primarily as an ironic commentary on Verdi's past achievements. That's certainly one way to attend to Verdi's last opera. But there are others, in this case a view that can celebrate the opera's startling discontinuities, causing us to imagine it looking forward: what is more, looking forward into a redrawn picture of Verdi's musical legacy, and ultimately a redrawn picture of the very nature of musical modernism.

After all, we've had a whole century now of the closing fugue, of "Tutto nel mondo è burla!" as the iconic message par excellence of late Verdi. It has the bright, uncomplicated C major with which the opera began; it might even be described as a recomposition of the opening motive of the first scene. The sense of an ending, a compact ending, a polyphonic farewell, has been with us and will remain with us. Yet anniversaries such as the one Verdi endured a few years ago present an opportunity for reassessment: they measure time and distance; in the words of the novelist Bernhard Schlink, they can act in "building bridges between the past and the present, observing both banks of the river, taking an active part in both sides."[31] In that spirit, then, we might substitute "Che giornataccia nera" for "Tutto nel mondo è burla!"; for a while at least, we might enjoy the changed landscape. It may of course be a merely temporary dislocation. The cliché of that old man with flowing scarf saying farewell to the nineteenth century with a smile and a song will probably flood back, doubtless aided in some small way by the deluge of trivia that "branded" the 2001 centenary. But for a while we could resist. The idea of Verdi, modernist in the seventh age of man, can also be attractive: the idea of him observing both banks of the river, knowing that one has receded for good.

Let me put this another way: in spite of its fragmentation, *Falstaff* is in many ways a rather untypical "late work"; it seems, for one thing, very far from inward looking. However, at the start of the last complete operatic scene Verdi wrote there is a gap through which we see another image. As never before, Verdi reached Act III, scene 1, to be confronted with an operatic work of his own making that was both finished and unsealed. In part he resorted to self-quotation to overcome the impasse, just as the aging Wagner had admitted privately that, in Act II of *Parsifal*, he had "taken up the old paint pot" and imitated the language of *Tristan*.[32] But at "Che giornataccia nera" Verdi did something different: as Falstaff bleakly examines his aging body, so his creator conjures up Klingsor, and along with that impotent, painted magician comes the specter of a musical future he will not live to witness.

The moral of this tale is rather different from that of my first three chapters. One might imagine performances that switched the orchestral preludes to *Falstaff* Act II, scene 1, and *Parsifal*, Act II, an operation that would certainly make audiences at Bayreuth sit up and take notice; but there is in truth little likelihood of enticing or outrageous substitutions, of external ways in which we can destabilize these operatic works. However, we might all the same ponder the fact that a late point in Verdi's last opera is marked by a curious incursion from another work. A question embeds itself, one perhaps made larger and more disturbing by knowledge of the compositional process and historical context that enfold it. True, a generous serving of *vin caldo* closes (at least temporarily) the wound in Falstaff's ego; but the appearance of a stagy magician, of pantomime sorcery, is for me, now, less easily brushed aside. There may be no easy, Adorno-like explanations to account for the presence of this strange musical detail; but it may nevertheless encourage us to think again about old oppositions: oppositions certainly between composers and their musical worlds; but also oppositions within the works they have created.

FIVE

Berio's *Turandot*

Once More the Great Tradition

I have caught
An everlasting cold; I have lost my voice
Most irrecoverably.

—Webster, *The White Devil*

THE LOST VOICE

On 1 September 1924 Giacomo Puccini was cautiously gathering his forces.[1] The end of *Turandot*, so long in sight but so frustratingly unattainable, now seemed possible. He wrote to his librettist and friend Giuseppe Adami:

> Today I'm starting to write again. I've passed through tremendous crises—with regard to my health as well as other things. The trouble in my throat, which has been worrying me since March, was beginning to look serious. I'm feeling better now, and have, moreover, the assurance that it's rheumatic in origin and that with treatment I'll be cured. But I've had some very black days. . . . Now I'll again start the work interrupted six months ago! And I hope soon to see the end of this blessed princess. At the moment my horizon is clearer in every direction.[2]

As he intimates, the final stages of *questa benedetta principessa* had been unusually protracted, even by Puccinian standards. The project, first mooted by Adami and Renato Simoni in March 1920, had gone through the usual agonizing genesis: endless prose and verse scenarios proffered and rejected; the predictable midstream crisis during which Puccini, having completed about half the opera, became convinced that it must radically change in overall shape; and then the last stumbling block. Everything up to the final scene was finished, fully orchestrated—had even been sent to the engravers—by the end of March 1924. But the closing duet between Calaf and Turandot, the moment that from the beginning Puccini had seen as the key to the opera, simply wouldn't come to life.[3]

A brief reminder of the background, and of what this scene entails, may be useful. The action of *Turandot* takes place in a distant, legendary China. In Acts I and II Calaf, an unknown prince, wins the icy Princess Turandot's hand in marriage by successfully answering three riddles. She wants nothing of him (or indeed of any man), and he magnanimously gives her an opportunity to escape: if she can discover his name by dawn, he will die instead of claiming her hand. The first scene of Act III, which begins with the famous tenor aria "Nessun dorma," stages the princess's frantic attempts to find this name. Calaf's blind old father, Timur, and Timur's slave girl assistant, Liù (who of course loves Calaf), are discovered; Turandot orders that they be tortured into revealing the name. Liù protects Timur by declaring that she alone knows the secret and then kills herself to avoid torture. The scene ends as Timur desolately departs with her funeral procession. The final scene is little more than a long duet between Calaf and Turandot. She at first continues to resist; but she capitulates after Calaf treats her to a long, violently intense kiss (patently symbolic of *the* unstageable operatic act). In a Tristan-like ecstasy of love-death-passion, Calaf then reveals his name to her. She summons the crowds; we believe she will utter the name and so cause his death; but at the last moment she announces, meltingly, that his name is "Amor." The opera ends in public rejoicing.

As was usual with Puccini, inability to compose did not on the surface involve musical problems: he occasionally admitted to purely musical difficulties—in *Turandot* he had experienced trouble with the opening scene of Act II—but for the most part music would flow reliably when he felt the libretto to be in order. And it was the verbal structure of this final scene with which he had been continually ill at ease. By December 1923 the duet had been through three drafts and was undergoing a fourth. By February 1924 the fourth version would not do; March, April, and May saw sporadic work and demands for yet more revisions. Then illness got the better of Puccini, and the summer was lost.

As his letter suggests, the beginning of September brought with it a sense of physical improvement and new energy. It was alas short-lived. Only a week later, Arturo Toscanini, who was to conduct the premiere of *Turandot*, visited Puccini and cast his own doubts on the ending, and so the rest of September was taken up with Puccini's requests for yet more verbal changes. This time his librettists, at least as he then saw it, hit on the right solution. On 8 October Puccini wrote to Adami that he had received some verses from Simoni (Adami's collaborator on the libretto), and that "they are very beautiful, and they complete and justify the duet."[4] He began working in earnest and in a matter of ten or so days had drafted twenty-three sheets of musical sketches: these covered most of the vocal lines—and a rudimentary, piano-score accompaniment—for approximately the first third of the scene, through the prolonged kiss and up to Turandot's words "La mia gloria è finita!"; but—perhaps revealingly—the actual moment of the kiss is missing. There are also several jottings for later moments, and clear indications in the libretto where earlier passages in the opera were to be recalled. But then, no more. By mid-October Puccini's throat disorder had been diagnosed as cancer. The truth was kept from him, but his decline was precipitate. On 4 November he moved to a clinic in Brussels where new X-ray treatments offered a last hope. An operation took place during which seven platinum needles were inserted into his throat. Puccini lost command of his voice, could no longer speak; he scribbled on a pad: "It feels as though I have bayonets in my throat; they have butchered me."[5] And finally, as the director of the institute said, "C'est le coeur qui ne résiste pas."[6] Puccini died of a heart attack on 29 November. The twenty-three sheets of sketches were all he left of the final scene of *Turandot.*

We do well to begin at the end because the unfinished work, particularly if interrupted by the death of its creator, has a peculiar aura in our culture. What is more, our fascination with things left unfinished may reveal something important about more general aesthetic attitudes. The revelation will not, though, be easy or straightforward, for our views seem to be channeled through a puzzling intersection of two competing allegories of temporality: one allegory is the story of the artist's life, a story inevitably bounded by the swift progress of some now-distant time; the other is the story of his work, which also inscribes time, though in a very different, in some senses more immediate way. The unfinished work is, in other words, at once "artistic" and "biographical"; it presents two levels of discourse, and the levels are not always compatible. On the one hand is a work whose temporal span is unnaturally foreshortened, whose lack of an ending marks it as forever imperfect. On the other hand, though, this very lack necessarily engages a further, equally exigent allegory of temporality, that of the composer's life history, which completes itself in the act of leaving the work unfinished.

Where opera is concerned, there is a further dimension to this confusion of endings and non-endings, one often used to mediate rather than further confuse the entanglements of work and biography. This is the dimension of "plot," the narrative that weaves around operatic drama. It is typical of the dominant trends in Puccini scholarship that, in the case of *Turandot,* this dimension has commanded extensive discussion. Many commentators, most notoriously Mosco Carner, have seen great significance in Puccini's failure to complete the final duet. Never one to feel embarrassment or hesitation at mixing Puccini's plots with what he liked to call the composer's "psychological mainsprings," Carner wrote that "Puccini's failure to complete this particular love duet cannot be merely ascribed to the onset of his tragic illness; it seems to have sprung from something deep down in himself, from obstacles in his unconscious mind."[7] Thus the knot is tied: life, work, and plot all huddle together under what Vladimir Nabokov enjoyed calling the stiff, black, Freudian umbrella.

Carner's is in many ways a comforting solution, one always likely to find disciples. Readers who have followed me this far will, though, guess that I want to advocate other routes by which we can depart from the idea of *Turandot* as a creative fragment, itineraries that can avoid simplistic connections between the life and the work. *Turandot* is in some obvious ways "finished": it has, for example, a complete libretto, approved by the composer; we thus know "what happens" in the final scene. Probably for this reason it was thought inevitable that Puccini's sketches, fragmentary though there are, should be realized and worked out by another hand. However, and as discussed briefly in the first chapter, the status of unstable works becomes especially contentious when some of the instability is created not by the author but by others. Ethical as well as aesthetic issues come to the fore. It was, then, probably inevitable that the completion of *Turandot* would from the start be a site of debate and dismay.

ALFANO'S SHAME

Puccini's publisher Ricordi commissioned a composer of the younger Italian generation, Franco Alfano, to complete the opera. *Turandot* received its first performance, conducted by Toscanini, on 25 April 1926, some year and a half after Puccini's death. On that first evening, Toscanini did not allow the Alfano ending to be heard. He stopped the opera after Liù's body and Timur departed the stage, announcing to the audience: "The opera ends here, because at this point the Maestro died."[8] After that first evening, though, and down to the present day, Alfano's ending has been an inseparable part of *Turandot*. As Alfano must have guessed, his connection with Puccini has assured him a prominence in operatic history that he would otherwise almost certainly lack. But the price was steep: his position in the pantheon has almost invariably been as a prime exhibit in the hall of shame.[9]

Criticism started even before those first performances. Alfano's first stab at the finale was 377 bars long, and (apart from that opening section of continuous sketches and from reminiscences dictated by the text) it was defiantly an ending of his own composition.[10] Toscanini insisted that this version be substantially cut (by nearly a third), and that more attention be paid to Puccini's surviving sketches.[11] Alfano reluctantly agreed, but the revised version (the one almost always performed these days) has remained forever open to the same criticism. In matters of motivic recall Alfano was of course constrained to adopt at least an echo of the composer's voice: Puccini had, for example, already made it clear that he intended a grand choral reprise of "Nessun dorma" as the final gesture of the opera. But even in this final section, the manner of recall seems at times to draw attention to the motive's strange new surroundings.[12]

Orchestration, though, is at the center of the disparity between Alfano's and Puccini's musical vision. Amazing as it may seem, Alfano did not consult Puccini's full orchestral score while working on his conclusion. In common with others of his generation, he regarded orchestration as beyond his "philological" duties and made little or no attempt to adapt his technique to Puccinian practice. In short, and despite the fact that he used the libretto Puccini approved and some of those twenty-three pages of sketches, and despite the fact that he knew from the start that he should "not be too like Alfano,"[13] he nevertheless closed "Puccini's" *Turandot* with his own voice, as if clearly to announce his difference in generation and in cultural influence. The closing moments, following Calaf's revelation of his name, are a good case in point: the Cecil B. DeMille strings at their highest reach, the massive doublings, the Straussian horn passages; all put us in a world that is firmly a generation apart from Puccini's more discreet, and above all more nuanced, orchestral usage.[14] And the fact that these gestures culminate in a triumphant reprise of some of the best-known themes of the opera, melodic inventions that are now at least unmistakably Puccinian, creates no more than a further level of difference and disjunction between thematic material and instrumental context.

We might pause here on one further moment in Alfano's ending: the one in which Calaf kisses Turandot. As mentioned earlier, this critical juncture lacked a trace of Puccinian sketch. The final version of the libretto perhaps already betrays a problem, or at least a gap: rather than sung words tracing the transformation, we have an elaborate (and for modern eyes elaborately embarrassing) stage direction, one full of what might now be called fascist virility,[15] couched in the language of a genre of novel that I'm told is still called the "bodice-ripper":

TURANDOT
No! . . . mai nessun m'avrà!
Dell'Ava mia lo strazio
Non si rinnoverà!
Non mi toccar, straniero! . . . È un sacrilegio!

IL PRINCIPE IGNOTO
Ma il bacio tuo mi dà l'Eternità!

> *E in così dire, forte della coscienza del suo diritto e della passione, rovescia nelle sue braccia Turandot, e freneticamente la bacia. Turandot—sotto tanto impeto—non ha più resistenza, non ha più voce, non ha più forza, non ha più volontà. Il contatto incredibile l'ha trasfigurata. Con accento di supplica quasi infantile, mormora:*

TURANDOT
Che fai di me? . . . Che fai di me? . . .
Qual brivido! . . . Perduta! . . .
Lasciami! . . . No! . . .

IL PRINCIPE IGNOTO
Mio fiore,
Mio fiore mattutino . . . Ti respiro . . .
I seni tuoi di giglio
Tremano sul mio petto . . .

[TURANDOT: No! . . . no one shall ever have me! / My ancestor's torture / Will never be repeated! / Don't touch me, foreigner! . . . It is sacrilege! / THE UNKNOWN PRINCE: But your kiss gives me Eternity! / *And in so saying, strong in the knowledge of his rights and his passion, he seizes Turandot in his arms and frenetically kisses her. Turandot— confronted with such force—has no resistance, has no voice, has no strength, has no will. The incredible contact has transfigured her. In a begging,*

EXAMPLE 12. Franco Alfano's ending to Giacomo Puccini's *Turandot*, Act III: the kiss.

almost infantile tone, she murmurs: / TURANDOT: What are you doing to me? . . . What are you doing to me? . . . / What shudders! . . . I am lost! . . . / Leave me! . . . No! . . . / THE UNKNOWN PRINCE: My flower, / My morning flower . . . I breathe you in . . . Your breasts of lily / tremble on my chest. . . .]

Readers will be relieved to know that even Alfano found this prose a shade of purple too far and cut it radically. But, as you can also see from example 12, his musical realization of the scene is brief and violent to the point of brutality. The sketches tell us that Calaf's words "il bacio tuo mi dà l'Eternità" signal repetition of earlier music in the score. But then the missing kiss takes up a mere two measures: *Tristan*-like dissonance piles on dissonance and then releases onto a sequence of rhythmically irregular, triple forte bangs on the drum, bassoons, and trombones. If this is a representation of sex, then the act is a barbaric, messy business, overwhelmingly concerned with power. Although Alfano left out the stage directions, his music makes graphic the kind of sexual contact they adumbrate.

ENTER THE KNIGHT

Alfano's ending reminds us, to be brief, that Puccini's opera is in some ways redolent of an age and of attitudes we would rather forget. A glance at contemporary reactions to the opera makes this embarrassment abundantly clear: everyone loved Liù and her acts of female self-sacrifice and were generally confused by the protagonist. Adriano Lualdi, one of the leading lights of the burgeoning fascist cultural industry, summed up the attitude with awful certainty:

> The Prince has nothing else to do but embrace and feel the beautiful body of the basilisk-woman. Slapping her, beating her about would have been better. Certain women enjoy this sort of gentle persuasion. Perhaps Turandot was one of them. Had she in her turn become a victim, we would finally have been able to feel some sympathy for her.[16]

There is, I'm afraid, plenty more where that came from. If ever an opera was in need of rehabilitation from its reception (Alfano's included), *Turandot* was it. Had the work not been so popular (and money-spinning), and had not Alfano protected the publisher's and his own rights by surviving into robust old age (he died in 1954), someone would surely have attempted an alternative ending long before our own era.

Small surprise, then, that the looming certainty of *Turandot* entering public domain heralded the appearance of a modern knight, a savior well known for his attention to bereft, abandoned subjects. Luciano Berio (1925–2003) was of course a central pillar of the European postwar avant-garde, perhaps *the* central pillar, with Stockhausen ever more eccentric and Boulez entombed within IRCAM. Berio alone among the lions of the 1950s and 1960s found a broader audience, and in part he did so by creative involvement with music from beyond the concrete studio, from orchestrations, completions, and arrangements of composers as diverse as Monteverdi, Bach, Schubert, Verdi, Mahler, even Lennon and McCartney. His new completion of *Turandot* was premiered in Las Palmas in early 2002 and was later that year staged in Los Angeles, Amsterdam, and Salzburg. As befits such an event, Berio's *Turandot* has already produced an impressive volume of discourse, some trivial, some official, some splendidly detailed and scholarly, but most of it unashamedly celebratory. Firmly at the trivial end, and certainly in the minority so far as aesthetic judgment is concerned, was a lone punter at the end of an Amsterdam performance who shouted "Bravo Alfano."[17] Firmly at the scholarly end, and certainly the best account of Berio's new finale I have seen so far, is the young Italian scholar Marco Uvietta's long essay, part of which appeared in conjunction with the world premiere, and which benefited from some consultation with the composer.[18]

To my knowledge, though, no one has yet discussed what might be called the consistency of the claims made about and around Berio's ending. First, it is immediately obvious that in large sections of (necessarily) free composition Berio's musical language is radically different from Puccini's: like Alfano before him, Berio made little or no attempt to constrain his invention within the bounds of Puccinian harmonic or orchestral practice; so much so that in places he wrote in a musical language that Puccini would have found frankly incomprehensible.[19] Second, Berio stressed in interviews, and Uvietta has documented painstakingly, his careful study and conspicuous use of almost the full range of sketches left by Puccini, whereas—as we saw—Alfano discarded almost everything that lacked an obvious musical context.[20] Third, Berio also claimed to make (and has been applauded for making) better sense—better than the original libretto, and certainly better than Alfano—of some of the most notorious dramatic "problems" that we today, our modern sensibilities being what they are, find in the final scene. Here's an example of what Berio said on the topic:

> I believe that *Turandot* was left unfinished not because of Puccini's death but because he was betrayed by an intractable libretto: this oriental tale that reaches a "happy end" is of indescribable vulgarity, and that's what gave Puccini problems. . . . I have rethought the finale completely: no longer a "happy end" but a more open and reticent conclusion, an oriental vision of things, less deterministic, less obvious. . . . I have simplified, removed [from the libretto] the more vulgar things, always in accord with the musical concepts formed by my study of the sketches.[21]

In the range of his musical language, Berio inevitably increased the distance we feel between his completion and the rest of the opera. In another sense, though, he staked claims for the enhanced "authenticity" of his version by making fuller use of the composer's explicit (or at least concretely surviving) intentions (note in the quotation above that reference to alterations made "always in accord with the musical concepts formed by my study of the sketches"); and in yet another sense he boldly "reinterpreted" the work to suit contemporary sensibilities. Although Berio was in certain ways radical in his musical additions, he felt the need to be reverent, significantly so, before the musical objects Puccini abandoned (to scrutinize them carefully, include them, ponder them). Despite the style gap, there is a sense in which each sketch, musical aperçu, motif fragment, has a legitimacy and claim to some form of survival that the libretto and its sentiments (which were in one sense more strongly endorsed by Puccini) do not.

Stated thus baldly, these claims might seem interestingly contradictory; it might even be that the domains of ethics and aesthetics have been too easily, too seamlessly merged, that the idea of "authenticity," of what we might know of Puccini's intentions, has been treated with a certain lack of circumspection. There is, though, a clearer and less negative way of articulating the issue. Discussions of Berio's *Turandot* would benefit from taking more notice of the fact that the opera has, like all works of art, inevitably changed with the changing times. Now more than three-quarters of a century after the opera was created, we cannot ignore—to name only one changed circumstance—a vast mass of reception accumulated around it. One result of this admission would be to ensure that notions of authenticity, of a move back to "Puccini's" *Turandot*, cannot now easily be reconciled with notions of making the opera more acceptable to today's audiences.

We can explore these issues by way of three moments from Berio's completion. First its opening bars. The start of Puccini's sketches seems to offer a violent juxtaposition of key, orchestral sonority, and mood: the dirge-like, subdued E♭ minor of Liù's funeral cortege gives way to the stark fifths and octaves (in A minor) of "Principessa di morte." As example 13a demonstrates, Alfano if anything intensified the brutality of this sudden, unmediated shift to a new dramatic world; and the strident scoring and articulation (the strings are instructed to play "tutte sciolte e sempre accentate") merely underline the fact. By comparison, Berio's beginning (example 13b) softens the edges of this join by adding a fifteen-measure transition, all of Berio's invention—one that travels motivically from reminiscences of the immediate past to ideas from still earlier in the opera, and on to prominent hints of the "new" musical language to come, including gestures to the opening bars of Wagner's *Tristan* and some moments bordering on the atonal.[22] When "Principessa di morte" (and Puccini's sketch material) eventually arrives, it too is muted

EXAMPLE 13. Franco Alfano's and Luciano Berio's endings to Giacomo Puccini's *Turandot*, Act III: the beginning.

a. Franco Alfano

Rimangono soli, l'uno di fronte all'altro, il Principe e Turandot.
La Principessa, rigida, statuaria sotto l'ampio velo, non ha un gesto, non un movimento.

EXAMPLE 13 *(continued)*

b. Luciano Berio

(continued)

EXAMPLE 13 *(continued)*

(at least by comparison with Alfano's), the orchestral colors are softer, and that anomalous F♯ in the very first measure again mediates between the past and the future, adding to the A minor chord a sonority that will become of great importance later in the scene.[23]

There is much to admire in the delicacy of Berio's solution here, not to mention the economy of means that can establish so much that is musically important to the scene in so few bars. One might, though, still be nervous of pronouncing it an unambiguous, unarguable improvement on Alfano's version, still less a more "authentic" solution. Even on the most conventional stylistic grounds the addition may be open to question. Puccini may indeed have been famous for subtle transitions from one mood to another; but he was also famous for his ability (a decidedly un- and anti-Wagnerian ability) to articulate new stages in the drama by means of musical non sequiturs such as that found between the end of Liù's scene and the start of the sketches. As it happens, there is a significant example of this in Act 1 of *Turandot*, as the chorus disappears to leave Calaf, Timur, and Liù alone on stage (example 14)—significant in that the tonalities involved are exactly the same. More important, though, one could argue that the precipitate move from one scene to another is brutal, vulgar even, in order to make a very precise dramatic

EXAMPLE 14.   Giacomo Puccini, *Turandot,* Act I.

point: as in the Act I "break," it signals the start of an entirely new phase of the drama, one that makes better sense if understood violently to disregard the preceding stage action and musical atmosphere. According to this context, Berio's mediation might even be seen as a blurring of the opera's sharp edges, as casting a veil over its stark reality.

My second example is undoubtedly Berio's most radical difference from Alfano, at least in musico-dramatic terms. It occurs at the moment of that notorious, troublesome, transfiguring kiss. As we saw in example 12, even Alfano quailed at the libretto's scene directions here; Berio, however, dispenses with them almost entirely. Instead of those muscular bangs on the drum, he inserts a three-minute orchestral interlude, one clearly intended to inscribe time—to mark a process of transformation so conspicuously lacking in sung verbal terms. Puccini had in other operas indulged in such orchestral moments himself, of course: symphonic interludes were all the rage in Italy's Wagner-obsessed fin de siècle; even later, in *Madama Butterfly* and, perhaps closest in spirit to the present example, in the finale of *Suor Angelica*, he had used them to great effect. But in musical language Berio's interlude is of course like none of these (example 15).

Berio's modern "kiss" defines itself by means of stylistic heterogeneity, by its bold mixture of free composition, reminiscences of past music from the opera, "realizations" of fragments of sketch material, and quotes from the Austro-German past of Wagner, Mahler, and Schoenberg. The opening of the interlude is an example. First come three bars redolent of *Tristan.* Then comes a strangely worded scene direction, invented by Berio: "Il Principe abbraccia il corpo di Turandot" (the prince [Calaf] embraces the body of Turandot). The sexual overtone here was deliberate: no hint of a dead or lifeless body (one possible interpretation of the Italian) was intended; Berio was instead trying to hint that at this moment Turandot is both distancing herself from herself and "getting lost" in unexpected passion.[24] Above all, though, the point of view is that of Calaf; she has become "an object"; Calaf embraces not her but "her body" as object (obviously, carnal object). Over this scene direction come two measures of a Puccinian sketch fragment; then, starting at m. 78, there occurs a remarkable passage perhaps best described as a Joycean "birth of language" metaphor for gathering sexual passion. It starts with the same chord (an A minor triad with added F♯) that acts as a connective sonority through the entire scene (we saw it in the first measure of "Principessa di morte"), but then fleeting quotes from Mahler's Seventh Symphony (first movement, opening theme) and Schoenberg's *Gurrelieder* (a brief moment from part 1), both chosen because they resemble fragments of existing music in *Turandot*, contribute to tonal disintegration, all culminating (at m. 88) in a long drawn-out high B♭ (what we assume is "the kiss"). At m. 89 it sounds as though we're into the prelude to *Aida*, but then franker quotations from the *Tristan* prelude alternate with further

EXAMPLE 15. Luciano Berio's ending to Giacomo Puccini's *Turandot*, Act III: the kiss.

(continued)

EXAMPLE 15 *(continued)*

EXAMPLE 15 *(continued)*

(continued)

EXAMPLE 15 *(continued)*

sketch fragments (the latter are the diatonic passages, most startlingly at mm. 98–100) and further "motivicized" reminiscences from earlier in the opera (at m. 110, for example, a theme from Act 1 is contrapuntally mixed with the "Nessun dorma" motif, again in the context of that F♯–altered A minor triad).[25]

What are we to make of this recuperation of the kiss? On the most obvious level, one could imagine no greater contrast to those agitated scene directions in the original libretto. Stage action is relegated or rather ignored; if deeds of music are to be made visible, it will perforce be the task of the stage director; perhaps, then, we have a Wagnerian sense of drama to match the Wagnerian and post-Wagnerian musical visiting cards. In the process, or—better—as part of the process, a remarkable musical claim is made: for Puccini's connection to what is in some circles still thought of as the "central line" in early twentieth-century music history, the one leading from Wagner to Mahler to Schoenberg; and eventually, it has to be said, to Luciano Berio. That syntactically curious stage direction might here take on a new, non-authorized meaning. "Il Principe abbraccia il corpo di Turandot." Is Berio here embracing the body of *Turandot*, perhaps of Puccini himself? Is he trying to guide the composer into a new future, connect him to a past now grown old and in need of new resources?

My third, and last, "moment" from the finale as realized by Berio involves its final gestures. As mentioned earlier, Alfano took some hints from Puccini's sketches and ended with a massive choral reprise of the climactic phrases of "Nessun dorma." This is a gesture that, at least superficially, recalls earlier Puccinian practice: both *La bohème* and *Tosca*, for example, close with reprises of "big solo tunes" from earlier in the final act. But in both cases the reprises are orchestral, which arguably makes a big difference (I cannot think of a Puccinian example that features the choral reprise of music first heard from a soloist); what is more, none of Puccini's later operas ends so simply—one thinks in particular of the gentle, ambiguous closes of *La fanciulla del West* and *La rondine*. Alfano's ending has, of course, been much criticized not only for its musical brashness, but—perhaps more tellingly—for the way in which that brashness disperses all hint of the uncomfortable price that has been paid on the route to this "celebration": in the poster-like colors of Alfano's ending, thoughts of the death of Liù and the fate of Timur might seem thoughtlessly, callously banished by loud noise and the waving of flags.

Again, Berio has answered tellingly many of these objections. He does indeed follow Puccini's sketch instructions by including a reprise of "Nessun dorma," but, as can be seen from example 16, his final pages are anything but triumphant. A libretto-dictated reprise of existing music in praise of the old emperor ("Diecimila anni") is followed by a further passage of radical tonal disintegration: Turandot's final public admission of love for Calaf, although in the highest vocal register, is curiously unsupported and far from affirmative (as in that earlier, ambiguous stage direction, she is somehow abstracted from the proceedings). The opera then concludes with a long instrumental postlude, one that retreads much of the musical ground both of Berio's prelude and the "kiss" interlude. Contrapuntal play is again made of the theme that first introduced Liù and Timur in Act I (mm. 288–91); this shades delicately into the "Nessun dorma" theme, again elaborated contrapuntally—but in the shadowy, unemphatic mood in which that famous tune was introduced at the end of Act II (mm. 294ff.). In the final measures of the score, at the moment the stage directions indicate "a poco a poco buio totale," we linger on a last *Tristan* chord, this time at its initial Wagnerian pitch and with dynamic emphasis (m. 302). The last four measures are then launched by a final, tenebrous, bass clarinet quotation from Liù's Act III aria. The Wagnerian tone here is unmistakable, and is perhaps strengthened by the fact that the quotation bears an obvious semantic pointer: Liù's words when she first sang those notes were addressed to Turandot and were "L'amerai anche tu." And then the closing cadence, which (as example 17 demonstrates), and in spite of its Klangfarbenmelodie orchestration, is plainly an elaboration of Puccini's final completed bars in the opera, those that ended Act III, scene 1.

EXAMPLE 16. Luciano Berio's ending to Giacomo Puccini's *Turandot*, Act III: final moments.

(continued)

EXAMPLE 16 *(continued)*

EXAMPLE 16 *(continued)*

(continued)

EXAMPLE 16 *(continued)*

EXAMPLE 17. Giacomo Puccini's *Turandot*, Act III, scene 1: final bars of Puccini's completed score.

THE GREAT TRADITION

As we have seen, Alfano's completion of *Turandot* can certainly be accused of straying from Puccinian practice; but Berio's ending is a much bolder departure at almost every level. There are most obviously those passages in which he gives free rein to his composerly personality, offering us a musical surface that gestures powerfully to a classic "high modernist" tradition. But even those passages in which Puccini's ideas are reused elaborate his motives by means of a type of linear chromaticism that Puccini tended to avoid even in this, his most heterogeneous and modern-sounding score. What is more, the passages of dense thematic-motivic saturation involve a level of contrapuntal interweaving that is close to a Wagnerian, and post-Wagnerian, Austro-German surface, but again one Puccini had little time for (one might even say had painfully overcome) after the distant days of *Manon Lescaut*. And finally there are Berio's gestures, notably in the long "kiss" interlude and at the end, to a world of ambiguity, quotation, and fragmentation, one that seems as much a farewell to Puccini as to Liù, and that has no hint of the uncomplicated triumph Puccini had imagined and the libretto reflected.

What are we to make of all this? In sketching an answer, let's immediately set to one side the business of the composer's intentions for the scene, and this despite Berio's protestations, despite his obsessiveness about the musical fragments left by Puccini. It is surely more fruitful to approach the opera from the point of view of what it *is* rather than what it once was or might have been. But even with that perspective, the prospects are far from simple. For example, as I've already hinted more than once, it could be argued that Alfano's ending now, itself, offers a telling critique, albeit an unintentional one, of the values expressed in the libretto. By brashly emphasizing the contrasts and climaxes, by setting the "kiss" in an atmosphere of brutal violence, by putting the denouement into a brash atmosphere that jars strongly with the rest of the score, in all this Alfano's ending might now be thought to make abundantly clear that no amount of celebration, however noisy, can close this opera satisfactorily. According to this reading, the very stridency of his opening gestures, of his solution to the kiss, of his final pages, points eloquently to a failure to resolve satisfactorily. In Andrei Serban's much revived Royal Opera House production of the opera,[26] there is a famous, Brechtian *coup de scène*: as the chorus strikes up with that reprise of "Nessun dorma," Timur painfully drags Liù and her cortège across the stage one last time. This has been commonly thought an example of "deconstructive" staging, but it could also be taken as a suitably flamboyant confirmation of what Alfano's music has already succeeded in telling us.

In one sense, then, Berio's shades and transitions, his use of stylistic fragmentation to soften the edges, in particular his refusal to celebrate the values advanced in the libretto for the final scene, might achieve, and with much greater subtlety, the same message as Alfano's mediated through Serban. In that sense he might indeed "save" the opera, help it toward contemporary acceptability. Although there's no need to develop it here, his version could even reflect back on to performances of the rest of the score, his gentle reminiscences encouraging tenors to de-Pavarottize what "Nessun dorma" has recently become, to experiment with a Calaf less certain of his vocal virility. But in doing all this Berio could, of course, also be accused: of enclosing the drama in a protective frame that serves to make less evident some of its historically specific message; of veiling ways in which it reflects all too clearly what we now regard as the unacceptable face of the cultural ambience in play at the time of its creation. In short, by making the opera more palatable, he acted (unlike Alfano, unlike Serban) as the most timid among *Turandot's* godparents.

However, with the delicately ambiguous music that closes his completion before us, I am reluctant to end there. Berio's new ending to *Turandot* should, at this stage, surely be welcomed, celebrated, above all experimented with in performance. But let's make sure the celebrations are for the best reasons. In spite of the fact that Berio studied and made use of the composer's sketches, we do not have here a *Turandot* that more nearly approaches the authentic, that more completely expresses Puccini's intentions. We have instead a strong contemporary reading, one that leads the opera on its journey into the future. It is important not because it has in some way "saved" *Turandot*, but rather because it underscores the fact that we can indeed rethink operas by rethinking their music.

Those last four words recall the arguments of my first chapter, and perhaps some reiteration is in order. Well, why not rethink the music? We change it all the time, we in the real world, in actual performances, under pressure of the moment, because of the tools at hand. We transpose, abbreviate, reorchestrate; we offer synthesizer-assisted performances, piano-accompanied performances. Why is changing the music a bad thing? Is nothing to be gained by opening these scripts to more radical metamorphoses, especially since reverent museum performances are always available as recordings? The paradox is that, to the very degree that traditionalists become incensed by performances—which after all are ephemeral and unlasting, seen as less important by far than the immortal work—they are proving how much more the performances count, and how little the scripts do. The very adherence to the primacy of the work, the fierceness of its defense in the face of its metamorphoses in realization, says something about it as a pretext.

In this sense, *Turandot's* unstable ending might present us with a stepping stone. Far from thinking its textual issues now "solved," we can instead look forward with pleasure to future solutions (alas, now they will not be by Berio) to other "difficult" Puccinian scenes; ones such as *Manon Lescaut* Act IV, which the composer tinkered with endlessly, never quite happy; or the final scene of *Butterfly*, which some modern sensibilities find at least as distressing as the ending of *Turandot*. Puccini's last opera, interrupted as it was by the composer's death, is often thought the end of a great tradition, as the last Italian repertory piece in a line that goes back more than three hundred years. But Luciano Berio's ending might just be a beginning, the start of a great tradition, of a proliferation of new ways in which the music that lies at the center of operatic works might be reconfigured.

SIX

Sudden Charms

The Progress of an Aria

My final chapter addresses George Frideric Handel, and in particular an aria that occurs in the second scene of his opera *Rodelinda* (written for London's Royal Academy in 1725). The scene is laid, of all unlikely places, in a Milanese cypress grove, amid tombs of the Lombard kings. Enter Bertarido, one of those kings; but, disconcerting for him, also a name inscribed on one of those tombs. His throne has been usurped, he is believed dead, a monument has been raised to his memory; but he returns to his homeland in disguise, seeking his beloved wife, Rodelinda. After a lengthy, scene-setting instrumental prelude, Bertarido sings a recitative, and then an aria apostrophizing his long-lost spouse:

> Pompe vane di morte,
> Menzogne di dolor, che riserbate
> Il mio volto, e 'l mio nome, ed adulate
> Del vincitor superbo il genio altiero,
> Voi dite ch'io son morto,
> Ma risponde il mio duol, che non è vero.
>
> *Legge l'iscrizione.*
>
> "Bertarido fu re: da Grimoaldo
> Vinto fuggì; presso degli Unni giace.
> Abbia l'alma riposo, e 'l cener pace."

Pace al cenere mio? Astri tiranni!
Dunque finch'avrò vita,
Guerra avrò con gli stenti, e con gli affanni?
Dove sei amato bene?
Vieni l'alma a consolar!
Sono oppresso da' tormenti
Ed i crudi miei lamenti
Sol con te posso bear.

[Empty trappings of death, / Lying grief, you who preserve / My face, and my name, and flatter / The haughty spirit of the proud conqueror, / You say that I am dead, / But my sorrow replies that it is untrue. / *Reads the inscription* / "Bertarido was king: defeated by Grimoaldo / He fled; he lies dead amongst the Huns. / May his soul find rest, and his ashes peace." / My ashes find peace? You tyrant stars! / As long as I have life, / Must I do battle with hardship and troubles? / Where are you, my beloved? / Come and console my spirit! / I am weighed down with pain / And only with you can I ease / My harsh laments.]

As many will know, this aria has become one of the most famous in all Handel. Why such fame is bestowed on one piece of music rather than another has always to an extent remained mysterious, the combination of factors—inevitably both internal and external to the text—is too complex to be encompassed completely within our explanatory economies.[1] However, shots—even random shots—at an internal-evidence answer are still surprising in their absence, for this as for most other Handel arias, famous or otherwise. "Dove sei amato bene" has a perfectly conventional da capo form, and perhaps that's part of the problem. Handel scholarship has, with a few recent and notable exceptions, been much readier to see the great man's operas as ideally at war with the formal stereotypes of its age. This preference for formal difference, by no means unique to Handelians, comes in part from a lingering sense that generic contracts are most interesting when broken, particularly when broken by geniuses in possession of large implements (Richard Wagner is a perennial favorite here);[2] but it may also draw on our established

terms of formal reference, which make such moments of generic transgression comparatively easy to write about. In the case of Handel, for
example, commentators have tended to stop analyzing or delving when
the composer behaves himself formally, when he writes uncomplicated
da capo arias; benign or uplifting adjectives are often the refuge, allow-
ing discussion to move along to the next generic transgression.

In this sense it is true to type that the most august of Handelians have
written at length about "Dove sei amato bene" only to concentrate on a
curious, "form-breaking" moment of suture between recitative and aria;
a moment that is helpfully marked by another of twentieth-century
musicology's favorite concerns: signs of authorial revision. The case is
succinctly discussed in Winton Dean's and Merrill Knapp's monumen-
tal study of Handel's early operas, and their account is developed (albeit
with some significant modification) by Andrew Jones, who is the editor
of the critical edition of *Rodelinda*.[3] Initially, Handel followed his source
libretto, by Antonio Salvi, in having no aria for Bertarido in this opening scene; the deposed king enters, reads out and comments on the
inscription on his monument, and is then interrupted by the appearance
of another character. But Handel returned to the scene to insert an aria
and, in doing so, experimented with various ways in which it might
emerge from the preceding recitative.

The fact that the aria was "tipped in" to the score, as an afterthought,
may account for the strangeness, perhaps even incompetence of its text
from a narrative point of view. There is, to give the most glaring example, no clue in the preceding recitative as to the identity of the "sei" in
"Dove sei": a quite startling discontinuity, which surely came about
through oversight rather than design. What is more, the poetry of the
second part of the aria is odd indeed. My translation of "Ed i crudi miei
lamenti / Sol con te posso bear" does its best, and *beare* figures in the
eighteenth-century Italian lexicon: but the precise meaning is nevertheless awkward. Is it possible that the composer himself wrote the text?

Whatever the case, Handel clearly had multiple thoughts over the
somewhat shaky linguistic bridge that joins recitative to aria. At one point

EXAMPLE 18. George Frideric Handel, *Rodelinda*, alternative version of "Dove sei."

he fashioned a conventional end to the recitative and an eight-bar ritornello—although (interestingly for my purposes here) not one that introduces us to the first vocal theme (example 18). At another point (whether before or after is a matter of debate between the experts), he concocted the elided version reported at the start of example 19 (the one we tend to recognize, as it is the version reported in the old Chrysander complete edition), in which the recitative moves seamlessly into the aria, and in which the opening ritornello is truncated to only four bars, in the process being made even less allusive thematically. Jones, with the latest philological weight behind him, now believes that example 18 is the *Fassung letzter Hand*, and that version is what audiences heard at the recent run of Glyndebourne performances, which were based on Jones's edition;[4] Dean and Knapp, however, enshrined example 19 and did so with telling metaphors, as "one of Handel's master-strokes, achieved in his fourth grappling with this scene." They don't even hint at the fact that the composer was, at least at one point, evidently undecided about this moment: for them he was clearly always heading in a direction—it happens also to be their direction; that "grappling" and those "master-strokes" move us

EXAMPLE 19. George Frideric Handel, *Rodelinda*, "Dove sei."

(continued)

EXAMPLE 19 *(continued)*

EXAMPLE 19 *(continued)*

onward into a form-breaking future that modern scholarship knows all about.

When Dean and Knapp come to discuss the aria itself, this preoccupation with "formal structure" reaches a more detailed level. They deserve full quotation:

> The vocal line is an education in melodic architecture. The falling second that begins each of the first three two-bar phrases receives a slightly different emphasis on each occasion. Then, after generating a four-bar phrase [mm. 12–16], it is isolated in two single bars, each ending with a rest, on the key word "vieni." Slowly the tune gathers way, gaining momentum from a falling seventh and reaching its climax at bar 31 with the only top E in Bertarido's entire part, heightened by the fermata in the previous bar. A seven-bar ritornello brings the A section to a close.[5]

As far it goes, this account of the musical surface of the aria might be judged sensitive, even exemplary. Most readers of this book will have grown up with similar descriptive language (not to mention with the more systematic formal and analytical methods that have collected around it), and some (this author included) may continue to promote its currency by teaching students how to apply its terms to a broad repertoire of pieces.

However, it will I hope seem other than merely churlish to point out that Dean's and Knapp's account achieves its authority and coherence by radically restricting (in effect by ignoring) what is *achieved* by the intervals they describe so lovingly—by sidelining the interpretation of character, or situation, or what you will, that the music accomplishes. Dean's and Knapp's lesson, in the end, is the lesson: the vocal line is "an education in melodic architecture." To put this another way, their description engages in a radical decontextualization: it certainly offers us a *meaning* for the aria, but it constantly refolds that meaning back into musical terms. The metaphors might seem to gesture outward, to refer to another art form; but such figures are now so routine as merely to short-circuit back to preoccupations of musical form. To steal a phrase from T. J. Clark's extended meditation on modernist painting, Dean's and Knapp's narrative account of "Dove sei amato bene" certainly "dramatizes" the aria; but what it dramatizes principally is the music's autonomy.[6]

I labor this point for what is, in the end, a quite simple reason. Guided by motives that will become clear a little later, I want to explore avenues through which "Dove sei" might "mean" in broader terms; in particular to find a way of talking about the aria that involves the words it sets, and that explores how those words might allow us descriptive access to further levels of musical signification, in one sense more specific, in another less so. Look again at the text of the aria, in particular at the opening two lines of poetry (which supply Handel with his text for the entire "A" section of the da capo). Although on one level perfectly conventional, these lines are peculiar in advancing a kind of contradictory energy, one first hinted at in the recitative. There Bertarido compared the conventional closure on the inscription of his monument, "abbia l'alma riposo, e 'l cener pace" (may his soul find rest, and his ashes peace), with the violent agitation of his all-too-living flesh: he asks a question, "Pace al cener mio?," and offers a vehement reply. The aria text is again taken up with a question ("Dove sei amato bene?" / Where are you, my beloved?) and then "answers" this with a demand or a plea ("Vieni l'alma a consolar!" / Come and console my spirit!). Handel, though, immediately makes this sense of dialogue more complex by his setting of the first four bars, which in one way construes the first line of text, the question, as itself a fragment of dialogue: the first two words, "Dove sei," are musically isolated, followed by a questioning pause; "amato bene" then offers closure, a kind of answer.

Some of the extraordinary power of this aria might stem from the tension created both by that ambiguous vocal opening and by the strangely unemphatic shift into lyrical discourse that so occupied Handel. The opening ritornello (whether of example 18 or 19) seems, rather than initiating a new state, to be the continuation of a dialogue with the vocal line: a dialogue that the character then intensifies with his first utterance. From then on, "consoling" four-bar patterns are continually answered by anxious, questioning rhythmic fragmentation. More than this, the musical "questions" are generated by a prevailing uncertainty about the role of the voice vis-à-vis the orchestra, one that again is "thematized" by the opening ritornello and its ambiguous echo from the vocalist. Most obviously this tension collects near the close (look at mm. 28–31 of example 19), in which that opening ritornello attempts to reassert itself, only to be gently interrupted by the voice's insistent plea of "vieni," and then by a climactic vocal appropriation of the ritornello material, an explosion on high E that is also the climax of Dean's and Knapp's exploration. This climax is followed by the strings' response: two bars, subito forte, of the opening vocal material. The ending alerts us to the fact that something important has been exchanged during the troubled course of this aria, perhaps something as simple as melodic energy, but perhaps as specific as the gap between a character's sense of loss and the object that has caused that sense.

Of course, this kind of activity may not be unusual in certain types of Handel aria, but I'd like nevertheless to draw attention to mm. 16–20, in which the process of exchange is at its most subtly disruptive. Together, voice and accompaniment could have made a four-bar phrase, and for the only time in the aria first violins and voice are in unison; but that disruptive, harmonically strange vocal repetition of "vieni" at m. 18 upsets the potential concord once more and leads the way to (perhaps calls for) the grander exchange at the close, already discussed. Think of the words again: "Dove sei amato bene? Vieni l'alma a consolar!" (Where are you, my beloved? Come and console my spirit!). On the smallest scale the aria is indeed made up of "calming," "consoling" musical gestures, of comforting closure. But there is an underlying question that will not go away, one that writes itself onto the large-scale rhythm of the piece but also speaks through the dialogue between voice and accompaniment. What, in the end, is the melody of "Dove sei"? And who articulates it? when? In the end, and to recall the divided energy of that opening couplet; perhaps part of what makes this aria so compelling is that it resists characterization, refuses to settle the question of whether it is about consolation or about the quest for consolation. In that sense the fact that Handel tinkered with the opening, leaving us with competing texts at the very moment at which the aria defines itself as a formal unit, is a potent symbol of what it is striving to achieve.

I have, as already mentioned, proposed this reading of "Dove sei amato bene?," one rather distant from that usually directed at Handel arias, as a way of expanding the aria's meaning, in particular of explaining how it might engage more interestingly with its verbal text. I don't pretend to have gone very far along that route, let alone to have escaped completely the more common terms of musical description, those short-circuit metaphors I mentioned a little earlier. What is more, the dangers of such close reading are plain. Most obviously, the generic context of Handelian opera constantly threatens to undermine such elaborations, not least because Handel was at times a magnificently cavalier word-setter. Worse still, the reading might even be thought to encourage a delving into the psychic personality of this Handelian character and thus to involve a violent and culturally arrogant assumption that today's idea of what makes an interesting or moving character must necessarily have been the project of this eighteenth-century sensibility. However, even with all this admitted, I want nevertheless to hold on to my reading for a moment: it will, if nothing else, help to negotiate some further Handelian pasts.

At the start of this chapter, I described "Dove sei" as one of the most famous arias in all Handel. That is true enough: the library catalogs will bear it out, listing as they do numerous reprintings of the aria from the late eighteenth century to the present day. However, a glance at such catalogs will immediately bring us to a crux, because if we examine that fame at all closely, it becomes clear that we have up to now been scrutinizing the wrong text. "Dove sei amato bene" largely disappeared, along with the rest of Handel's operas, soon after its first appearance; by far the greater part of the aria's reception history has instead been provoked by its manifestation in other, strikingly different guises. *Rodelinda* the Italian opera remained unstaged from the 1730s until its German revival during the so-called Handel-Renaissance of the 1920s, and it appeared then in a much altered, unashamedly Wagnerized version by the aptly named Oskar Hagen.[7] "Dove sei" continued to have some circulation as a self-standing Italian aria.[8] But increasingly it was displayed in borrowed robes. In the late eighteenth century and (particularly) in the nineteenth century, it mostly made the rounds as "Holy, Holy, Lord God Almighty," which—if we can judge by the number of editions—rivaled Mendelssohn as staple fare in the Victorian parlor.[9] Around 1905 the redoubtable Ebenezer Prout "edited" a version nearer that of Handel's original, or at least one that replaced "Holy, Holy" with an English translation of the original Italian.[10] And then, around 1910, came a further immensely popular version, "Art Thou Troubled?," which some readers may still remember. It remains in currency both in the backwaters of the British choral scene and—as we shall see—in postcolonial landscapes some distance beyond that.[11]

Charting as they did Handel's "grappling with this scene," a metaphor that closes the composer's fist quite closely around his text, it is hardly surprising that Dean and Knapp are unequivocal about the aria's rich and unruly proliferation over historical time. They tell us that "[Handel's] wonderful melody was spoiled for generations of listeners by association with inappropriate words, sacred and secular, dubbed by insensitive parodists beginning in Handel's day. It can only be fully appreciated in its context."[12] Given the broad aim of their book, and given the fact that these authors' Handelian past had been occupied almost exclusively by arrangements such as "Art Thou Troubled?," it would be unfair to linger over the wording here: to question, for example, what the authors could possibly have meant by "fully appreciated." In our more plural (I do not say "liberated") context, it may be more fruitful instead to risk "spoiling" Handel's melody by looking in some detail at the last of these efforts: not then at "Dove sei amato bene?," words by Nicola Francesco Haym; but at "Art Thou Troubled?," words by W. G. Rothery, and music (well, most of it) by a man *The New Grove Dictionary* continues proudly to proclaim "English composer of German birth." Mr. Rothery (about whom I've been able to discover no background whatsoever) was responsible for quite a few of these transformations; distributed energetically by the publisher Novello, they lasted and spread extraordinarily well.[13] Of course, putting English words to vocal music conceived in another language has rarely been a grateful task, particularly if the translator feels at all obliged to follow the sense of the original; it is, then, probably fortunate that, in fashioning an English version of "Dove sei amato bene?," Rothery made no attempt to translate from the Italian: instead he supplied a text entirely of his own making (example 20).

As a glance will show, this latter-day ode to St. Cecilia exhibits a pretty formidable collection of poetic tropes. One obvious reference is to a poet close in time to Handel (at least I assume that the opening lines have a deliberate echo of Congreve's "Hymn to Harmony"):

(continued)

EXAMPLE 20 *(continued)*

> Music alone with sudden charms can bind
> The wand'ring sense, and calm the troubled mind.

Perhaps this was even a gesture toward "period authenticity." More immediate, though, are echoes of John M. Neale's famous nineteenth-century hymn, which is itself a biblical trope:

> Art thou weary, art thou troubled,
> Art thou sore distressed?
> "Come to me," saith One, "and, coming,
> Be at rest."[14]

Whatever the case, those images of a music calling with voice divine, healing sadness at her shrine, seem to have at their base a conception far from Handel's: music is now, as befits a new age and new aesthetic sensibilities, a source of the ineffable, with a divine power that, while it may indeed soothe the savage breast, more tellingly vibrates in the memory.

What about the notes that clothe this evocation of music's mysterious power? As example 20 illustrates, Handel has also been *written over;* less radically perhaps than did Rothery, but nevertheless with some energy. There are the usual small-scale *aggiornamenti*, doubtless effected so as not to corrupt the harmonic habits of the young: Handel's spikily expressive voice-leading is smoothed out, Mendelssohnian sevenths are added, some Bach-chorale-like passing notes are sketched in, "doubled thirds" are avoided. More basic though, what I described as that enlivening tension between the vocal line and the accompaniment is sharply diminished: the accompaniment is now ubiquitous; the opening ritornello is tonally closed and shorn of its vocal prelude. Most radical of all, what I earlier pointed to as a nexus of rhythmic disjunction—at mm. 16–20—has now disappeared by the most draconian of means: that disruptive measure of anxious vocal repetition has simply been omitted.[15]

We have aesthetic choices when confronted by this new, very much "Englished" Handel. The easy way, the way of seeming certainty, is to dismiss it, see both its poetic and musical alterations as simply error: clean the picture of these accretions, get back to the original, a place where our interpretation can plausibly claim the authority of the composer, thus pretending to a kind of uninflected (even uninfected) history. Attractive as these fantasies of a tabula rasa might be, we need periodically to remind ourselves that they are both impossible and undesirable. The "impossible" is easy: any historian more than dimly aware of his discipline's philosophies will admit to that much. The "undesirable"—the idea that such goals might be a negative, a source of damage—is more contested. Winton Dean and Merrill Knapp powerfully represent the plain reconstructionist faith and would surely find my questioning of it somewhere between capricious, nonsensical, and heretical. And they are abetted or enabled by their formal description of the aria's "melodic architecture"—any change must of course damage their meaning for the aria, their dramatization of the music's autonomy. As you can guess, though, I want to suggest an alternative route: error there may be, perhaps even simple error, in Rothery's manipulations; but as we know, and as Frank Kermode has movingly argued, the history of interpretation is in large part a history of error—of a glorious enmeshment in contingency: we need to learn to use and benefit from multiple readings, not reject them.[16] To put this another way: the manipulations of text and music in "Art Thou Troubled?," however fortuitous the process that caused their creation, have produced something that many have valued and continue to value; the new object has its own, substantial reception, its own history.

Just as important, though, this new history is one that my earlier reading of "Dove sei" can take part in. As you see, Rothery certainly leaned on what we might call a musico-linguistic aspect of Handel's opening line, its suggestion of an embedded question-and-answer, what I earlier called a fragment of dialogue; and he made it much more explicit: "Art thou troubled? Music will calm thee." This new explicitness changes the landscape somewhat but does so in what can be thought interesting ways. Consider, for example, that final, lingering vocal pause on the word "music" (at m. 29), and then the achievement of the orchestral ritornello at the words "Music calleth with voice divine." The exchange of melodic competencies at the close, which I discussed in relation to "Dove sei," retains some powerful currency in this version, perhaps even accumulates meaning. It is certainly inflected differently, adapts to another age and another aesthetic; but "Dove sei" allows room for such change. More than this, part of the later aria's effect, its peculiar poignancy and sense of nostalgia, has been born out of the business of its creation, the fact that "Art Thou Troubled?" was produced by this process of *writing over* history, by inscribing the idea of "music" onto an alien musical text so strongly that another text was created.

I could at this stage expand on those last points, even offer a more detailed reading of "Art Thou Troubled?" to build further on that bestowed on its Italian sister, but it is more important and fitting to mention two stray moments from the reception the English version has engendered. One is personal and happened in September 2000 in the Eastern Cape region of South Africa, at Fort Hare University, which had the most dilapidated music department I have ever seen (it was quite literally on the verge of physical collapse), and which seemed to me sustained largely by the awe-inspiring energy and belief of one beleaguered teacher, the ethnomusicologist Dave Dargie. Among the things I found out there, quite by chance, was that "Art Thou Troubled?" remains a great favorite of the choral repertory in some parts of South Africa. A sometime choir director called Mavis Noluthando Mpola, visiting the campus as I was, and hearing about my interest in the piece, sung some strains of it from memory and later furnished me with the text commonly used by choirs in her region.[17] It was again under the imprint of Novello, but this time "arranged as a Four-part Song by H. A. Chambers," and entirely in tonic sol-fa notation. This, then, is how "Art Thou Troubled?" continues its progress in one part of the globe: in a notational form that reflects the presence of a tradition still largely oral. Perhaps once an item in the imperial march of progress, the aria-turned-song-turned-chorus has lived through hard times but is now thoroughly assimilated into local practice—Mpola was confident she could locate versions of the piece in Zulu or Xhosa; it has, in other words, taken its place beside the compositions of Reuben Caluza and others, part of that rich legacy left by an eighteenth-century gentleman whom, in another world, with other priorities, *The New Grove Dictionary* might call "South African composer of German birth."[18]

My second moment of reception brings us back to more familiar territory. It comes in the form of a recording made more than half a century ago, on the evening of 27 February 1946 in London's Kingsway Hall to be precise, by Kathleen Ferrier, accompanied by the swooping strings of Dr. (very soon to be "Sir") Malcolm Sargent and the London

Symphony Orchestra, a band that, in those pre-historical performance days, was innocent of the hemiola.[19] I treasure the recording for many reasons, but in this context the achieved serenity of Ferrier's negotiation of the da capo repeat is what I want to stress. The first "A" section does indeed stage a kind of rhythmic battle, but it is not so much between voice and orchestra as between Ferrier and her conductor: Sargent wants the tempo one way, she (as is evident from her very first, impatiently anticipated entry) wants it another. But by the reprise—proper to the manner of the day, one varied through dynamics, speed, and tone rather than through the melodic ornament we expect to hear today—I like to think that the sheer beauty of Ferrier's delivery, the sadness in the way she "heals thy sadness," above all the music in the way she sings "music," have finally soothed the savage breast, softened rocks, and bent the knotted oak; she has, to put it more prosaically, made Malcolm Sargent sit up and listen. By this means, an unlikely rapprochement is achieved; yet another text is created, this time a recorded one; one that has entered my imagination and will sit happily in the presence of "Dove sei," unlikely to be banished simply by the claims of authenticity.

The personal creeps in as this chapter, as this book, comes to an end; it is time to spell things out more clearly. We have encountered in "Dove sei" a musical object that has been treated to a peculiarly strong reception, so much so as to create a further text, one that I think is worthy of separate aesthetic contemplation. We could leave it at that and see the ideas explored in this chapter simply as a gentle warning: we can lose sight of precious objects and so deny ourselves much pleasure if we indulge in a musicology that is aggressively supply-side, that automatically and habitually privileges creation over reception. It may in this sense seem as though the chapter's relationship to my main theme in this book is obscure. In the strictly textual sense, it is; I don't imagine "Art Thou Troubled?" turning up in Glyndebourne's next run of *Rodelinda*, although stranger things have happened on the operatic stage. But in another, broader sense, the issues raised here are crucial to my project and can act as its conclusion.

My arguments in this book about Donizetti, Verdi, Mozart, Puccini, and now Handel have—by means of many close readings—returned periodically to the business of textual authority, to the matter of what we can know about works from the traces that have been left of them. It will probably be clear that I enjoy delving into philological and historical detail almost as much as I enjoy the music that emerges from within the marbled exteriors that protect autographs and other material traces. But there's always the Apthorpe problem. Evelyn Waugh's celebrated comic character was rich in peculiar detail—his porpoise-skin boots, his friend on good terms with gorillas—but tended to become faceless and tapering the closer he approached. The closer we look into the documents that carry works to us, the less distinct they become; the more we understand about the material traces, the more we feel encouraged, perhaps even empowered, to ignore their dictates. The sheer contingency of the material trace presses, makes us look outside the library window, along the route the music traveled.

One final homily. I've earlier quoted from Bernhard Schlink's novel *Der Vorleser* (in English, with an inevitable loss of nuance, it's known as *The Reader*), which involves a complex quasi-autobiographical investigation of the aftermath of the Holocaust. There is much talk about "doing history," in this case coming to terms with a past that was at first literally unthinkable. Schlink describes this dance to the music of time in architectural terms, as "building bridges between the past and the present, observing both banks of the river, taking an active part in both sides,"[20] and his metaphor keeps reappearing. His history is a business that actively engages the present in interpreting the past, indeed that sees the past as relevant only in terms of the present. Engaging with "Dove sei" and "Art Thou Troubled?" has elements of this merry-go-round: we are confronted with a multiform piece enfolding a clash of two sensibilities, nearly two centuries apart; the later object gains strength and a peculiar resonance from the sheer boldness of its appropriation of the past. If we automatically ignore such boldness, dismiss it as "mere error," or "inauthentic," or what you will, our vision of the past is sadly diminished. And perhaps that also means that we ourselves become diminished or at least becalmed. It is salutary to ponder the fact that some of these objects, after all, are from our own past and inhabit a world from which we cannot separate ourselves. We do well to gaze periodically at them as we complete our own, very partial progress.

NOTES

CHAPTER 1. REMAKING THE SONG

1. Tracking in detail the emergence and consolidation of this repertory, a process whose speed varied markedly from country to country, is a task largely still awaiting operatic scholars. There is, though, agreement about certain watershed periods. In the case of Italian opera, the political upheavals of the nineteenth century were of particular importance. As John Rosselli put it with his usual economy and grace, "Italian opera had been closely bound up with the world of the old sovereigns. It was shaken when the 1848 revolutions shook their rule; when, in 1859–60, they departed for good, Italian opera began to die." See Rosselli, *Music and Musicians in Nineteenth-Century Italy* (London, 1991), 71. For a detailed consideration of another watershed, the "opera crisis" of 1920s Germany, see Gundula Kreuzer, "'Zurück zu Verdi': The 'Verdi Renaissance' and Musical Culture in the Weimar Republic," *Studi verdiani* 13 (1998): 117–54, esp. 144–54.

2. For a prolonged meditation on this topic, one that has greatly influenced my formulations here but goes far beyond them in scope, see Carolyn Abbate, *In Search of Opera* (Princeton, 2001).

3. The production was first performed at Glyndebourne on 23 June 2002. It was conducted by Mark Elder and directed by Richard Jones.

4. For more on the progress of this movement in 1920s Germany, see Kreuzer, "Zurück zu Verdi," 146–48. For a succinct account of the rise of the

opera director, see Roger Savage, "The Staging of Opera," in *The Oxford Illustrated History of Opera*, ed. Roger Parker (Oxford, 1994), 350–420, esp. 387–401.

5. Richard Taruskin, *Text and Act: Essays on Music and Performance* (Oxford, 1995). I should also mention a recent, as yet unpublished essay of Taruskin's, at present entitled "Setting Limits," which concerns itself partly with these matters but also discusses at length issues central to the present chapter, in particular the case of "radical" stagings of opera that nevertheless remain, in Taruskin's words, "scrupulously compliant with what the composer had written." My thanks to Professor Taruskin for sharing with me a copy of this paper prior to publication.

6. Taruskin, "Setting Limits," makes a similar point more trenchantly when he asks "Why no techno *Traviata*s or R&B *Götterdämmerung*s?"

7. Lydia Goehr, *The Imaginary Museum of Musical Works: An Essay in the Philosophy of Music* (Oxford, 1992); mention should also be made of Roman Ingarden's *The Work of Music and the Problem of Its Identity*, trans. Adam Czerniawski, ed. Jean G. Harrell (Berkeley and Los Angeles, 1986), written in 1928 but causing considerable discussion when it appeared in English translation.

8. Goehr, *The Imaginary Museum*, 113.

9. Richard Middleton, "Workin(g)-Practice: Configurations of the Popular Music Intertext," in *The Musical Work: Reality or Invention?*, ed. Michael Talbot (Liverpool, 2000), 59.

10. Strohm goes on to state that the entire project "dovetail[s] with many other reificatory characterisations of the last 200 years . . . an abominable father's age, the enlightenment/modern age (after 1800), is contrasted with a happy grandfather's age, which had retained contact with the pastoral traditions of the rest of the world, until alienation through enlightenment and the work-concept took place." See Reinhard Strohm, "Looking Back at Ourselves: The Problem with the Musical Work-Concept," in *The Musical Work*, 151.

11. Michael Talbot, editor of the book of responses to Goehr, is for example bizarrely assured of the centrality of his discipline to the broadest matters of musical taste. In an account of the relationship between the work-concept and what he calls "composer-centredness," he notes that "performer-centred," single-artist recorded anthologies are now "increasingly viewed as naïve, at least in those countries where musicology impinges on musical life." See Michael Talbot, "The Work-Concept and Composer-Centredness," in *The Musical Work*, 176–77.

12. For a (very brief) discussion of operatic works, see Goehr, *The Imaginary Museum*, 216–17.

13. Goehr, *The Imaginary Museum*, 216.

14. In an answer to Strohm, Goehr develops this point, although again (defending her "watershed") espousing an earlier date than some think defensible. She suggests that "around 1800 texted music changed in the matter of text-note priority, and even in its conception, after music came to be defined primarily as the symphonic art of purely instrumental tone." See Goehr, "'On the Problems of Dating' or 'Looking Backward and Forward with Strohm,'" in *The Musical Work*, 241.

15. McGann's manifesto can be found at www.iath.virginia.edu/public/ jjm2f/rationale.html; its endnotes cite several of the key recent publications in this large debate.

16. Zachary Leader, *Revision and Romantic Authorship* (Oxford, 1996).

17. Leader, *Revision*, 4–5.

18. For meditations on this topic stimulated by a very different author, see Michael Wood, *The Magician's Doubts: Nabokov and the Risks of Fiction* (Princeton, 1995). I am particularly thinking of 11: "Like the rest of us, authors die at least twice. Once physically, once notionally; when the heart stops and when forgetting begins. . . . But there is another death of the author, most famously chronicled by Roland Barthes in an essay of 1968 and modelled on the death of God. To die in this sense is to be unmasked as a fiction, as a figment of faith. 'Death' reveals that there has been no life, only a dream of life."

19. Johanna M. Smith, in the volume devoted to *Frankenstein* in Case Studies in Contemporary Criticism (Boston, 1992), 274; quoted in Leader, *Revision*, 168.

20. Leader, *Revision*, 167–205.

21. In the paragraph that follows, my thanks above all to Hannah Ginsborg, whose generous dissection of a first draft of my arguments came at just the right time.

22. The Bergamo performances, conducted by Gustav Kuhn, produced by Beni Montresor, were given as part of Bergamo's Celebrazioni donizettiane. The CD, conducted by John Neschling, is available on the BMG Ricordi label, no. 2029. As ever, a most readily available source of information about the opera remains William Ashbrook, *Donizetti and His Operas* (Cambridge, 1982), especially 156–59.

23. They are collected together in MS 4060, with many other Donizetti materials, in the Malherbe Collection; my thanks to Gabriele Dotto and then Michel Noiray for furnishing me with copies of the pages relating to *Adelia*.

24. Letter to Antonio Vasselli, [Paris], 12 November [1842]; cited in Guido Zavadini, *Donizetti: vita—musiche—epistolario* (Bergamo, 1948), 452.

25. Donizetti's Italian for the last phrase is worth recalling: "Quando il soggetto piace, il core parla, la testa vola, la mano scrive"; letter to Antonio Dolci, Paris, 27 November [1842]; Zavadini, *Donizetti*, 455.

26. When *Maria di Rohan* was finished he mentioned that it had cost him "eight days of work, exactly eight days"; letter to Antonio Vasselli [Paris, 4 January 1843], in Zavadini, *Donizetti*, 464. Donizetti adds: "Please don't spread abroad my secrets: either the public won't believe it, or they will imagine that it's just scribbled-out music. Imagine a composer scribbling things down for Paris and Vienna!"

27. Such examination will have to await publication of the *Adelia* edition, but a preliminary description, together with an early version of some of the discussion that follows, appears in "Canonic Variations: The 'Rediscovery' of *Adelia*," in *Il teatro di Donizetti II: Percorsi e proposte di ricerca*, ed. Paolo Cecchi and Luca Zoppelli (Bergamo, 2004).

28. A more detailed examination of figure 1 would reveal still further versions, as there are numerous places in which individual phrases are themselves altered or furnished with alternatives. An example of such supplementary revisions can be seen on the right-hand side of line 10.

29. We should not make too much of this absence of text: the evidence of the sketches generally suggests that, at these early stages, Donizetti had the text before him but notated it only when issues of scansion might be in doubt.

30. When I initially presented some thoughts about this sketch at a Donizetti conference in Venice (the proceedings of which have now appeared; see note 27), most of the ensuing discussion was indeed taken up by participants who wanted to "narrativize" the progression from one sketch to another, although if memory serves me no one mentioned the gathering directness of utterance. Much was made of the "uncomfortable" splitting of "io" in all but the "definitive" version. Scholars sitting in Venice in 1997 seemed not to notice the irony of their spotting basic lapses in Italian word setting that Donizetti, who by 1840 knew a thing or two about such matters, had found acceptable enough to write out several times and even work into an orchestral score.

CHAPTER 2. OF ANDALUSIAN MAIDENS AND RECOGNITION SCENES

1. The term *trilogia popolare* does not appear in one of the earliest and most widely disseminated biographies, that by Arthur Pougin, although the three

operas are grouped together in a single chapter and are described as "the three operas by the composer that made him more popular"; see the "definitive" Italian version of Pougin's biography, *Giuseppe Verdi: vita anedddotica . . . con note ed aggiunte di Folchetto* (Milan, 1881), 67. The earliest example of the phrase I have found is in the Italian version of Camille Bellaigue's book on the composer, *Verdi: biografia critica* (Milan, 1913), 25, where it serves as a chapter heading; previous sightings, though, may well be possible.

2. It is generally accepted that *the* earliest opera thus to be blessed is Rossini's *Il barbiere di Siviglia*, to be followed by a handful of Bellini and Donizetti works. Earlier operas, notably some famous and long-lived examples in the French tradition, had been continuously performed (in their local strongholds, at least) through much of the eighteenth century, but they did not survive into the nineteenth. The most popular of Mozart's operas established brief repertory status in early nineteenth-century England, Germany, and France but then faded in the face of changing fashion. For an in-depth account of the demise of one such opera in one country, see Emanuele Senici, "'Adapted to the Modern Stage': *La clemenza di Tito* in London," *Cambridge Opera Journal* 7, no. 1 (1995): 1–22.

3. This last pairing belongs to Julian Budden, *The Operas of Verdi: From "Il trovatore" to "La forza del destino"* (London, 1978), 125. He continues: "Both speak the same language of melody, but what is virile and expansive in the one is feminine and intimate in the other."

4. Abramo Basevi, *Studio sulle opere di Giuseppe Verdi* (Florence, 1859; reprint, Bologna, 1978), 230.

5. Perhaps not by chance during this period of intense creative change, Verdi's two previous operas, *Stiffelio* (1850) and *Rigoletto* (1851), also touch each other in biographically and musically interesting ways. For more on this, see my "Lina Kneels, Gilda Sings," in *Leonora's Last Act: Essays in Verdian Discourse* (Princeton, 1997), 149–67, a chapter that in some ways takes on the role of less radical twin vis-à-vis the present piece.

6. *Il trovatore*, ed. David Lawton, appears in *The Works of Giuseppe Verdi*, series 1, volume 18A (Chicago-Milan, 1993); *La traviata*, ed. Fabrizio Della Seta, series 1, volume 19 (Chicago-Milan, 1997). My account of the genesis of the two operas is largely based on the historical introductions to these volumes.

7. Verdi probably saw the play in Paris in early 1852 and is usually thought to have been behind the idea of setting the subject; it is possible, though, that Piave was the first to consider the play's operatic possibilities. See Della Seta's introduction, xiii–iv.

8. See Lawton's introduction, xxii–xxiii.

9. Letter to Vincenzo Luccardi, 14 December 1852; quoted in Della Seta's introduction, xv.

10. Benjamin Lumley, *Reminiscences of the Opera* (London, 1864), 395–96, where the information is delivered in the form of a footnote. "In the course of this interview [in 1857 in Paris], Verdi told me that he had composed the 'Trovatore' in ten days and the first act of the 'Traviata' in four days, at Genoa, where he was detained by stress of weather, and remained *incog.*" In this context, "composed" would clearly mean "sketched"—at most in continuity draft. If Lumley can be trusted, it is interesting that Verdi was happy to boast of the speed at which he could compose; so different from Donizetti some years earlier (see the letter quoted on page 15, above). Perhaps, though, Verdi the spin doctor was already at work, consolidating with anecdote the mythic status of what was fast becoming the *trilogia popolare.*

11. Fabrizio Della Seta, ed., *Giuseppe Verdi: "La traviata": Schizzi e abbozzi autografi* (Parma, 2000). Della Seta's *Critical Commentary* on the sketches has subsequently appeared (Parma, 2002).

12. We must, it seems, deduce that Germont departed minutes before merely to take a scenic turn around Violetta's garden, perhaps to refuel his patriarchal authority after his harrowing confrontation with the heroine.

13. Della Seta, *Schizzi e abbozzi autografi*, 50, suggests this hypothesis in his description of the bifolio; see also his *Critical Commentary*, 177.

14. James Parakilas has discussed the "Parisian" aspect of this scene and suggests that a boldly ironic message is to be read from it: these divertissements are, he thinks, "a case of Verdi turning the tables, that the exoticized object here is, for once . . . the Parisians. These are Flora's rich Parisian friends, after all, masquerading as Gypsies and matadors, singing and dancing *à l'espagnole*, as rich Parisians were known to do. Would not Verdi's audiences have enjoyed this divertissement not simply as a put-on of the Spanish, but even more as a send-up of the Parisian put-on of the Spanish?" For me, this is a *Geheimnis* too far, though no less enjoyable for being so. See Parakilas, "How Spain Got a Soul," in *The Exotic in Western Music*, ed. Jonathan Bellman (Boston, 1998), 137–93, here 153.

15. To this list of melodic lookalikes could also be added "Ah, fors'è lui," the first movement of Violetta's Act I aria, which was initially sketched in E minor (see Della Seta, *Schizzi e abbozzi autografi*, 108–9).

16. The resemblance also plays out on a larger level, in that each example proceeds to a contrasting section in the parallel major.

17. Della Seta, *Schizzi e abbozzi autografi*, 44, draws attention to the use of what he calls these "neutral" keys, the most common of which are A minor,

E minor, and C major. As further sketch material emerges from the Villa Sant' Agata, it will be interesting to see how extensive is the use of such keys across Verdi's career, not least for the light it will shed on that once-contentious matter of Verdi's "tonal planning" within operas.

18. Della Seta's *Critical Commentary*, 146, mentions in passing the connection to "Stride la vampa," suggesting that Verdi revised the passage precisely in order to disguise it.

19. For a detailed exploration of the Spanish topos in Western music, see Parakilas, "How Spain Got a Soul"; as he says (152), "A book could be written about Verdi's Spains, and much of it would have to do with French mediations." Spanish local color is prominent in *Ernani* (1843), *Il trovatore* (1853), *La forza del destino* (1862), and *Don Carlos* (1867); a good pre-Verdian example, possibly one from which Verdi learned something of the style, is Donizetti's *Maria Padilla* (first performed at La Scala, Milan, in 1841, during the season that saw the premiere of Verdi's *Nabucco*).

20. For a classic illustration of this line of inquiry, see Harold Powers, "'La solita forma' and 'The Uses of Convention,'" *Acta musicologica* 59 (1987): 74–109; for a doubting postscriptum, see my "'Insolite forme,' or Basevi's Garden Path," in *Leonora's Last Act*, 42–60.

21. "Unheimlich sei alles, was ein Geheimnis, im Verborgenen bleiben solte und hervorgetreten ist." Sigmund Freud, "The 'Uncanny,'" in *Art and Literature*, ed. Albert Dickson, The Penguin Freud Library (London, 1985), 14:345. This chapter's epigraph is on 359.

22. I take the term *parlante* from Basevi, *Studio sulle opere di Verdi*, 220. He is rather dismissive about the episode and seems not to recognize the connection between the two halves of example 5: "The *terzetto* between Azucena, the count, and Ferrando is none too beautiful. Again here Azucena begins with a $\frac{3}{8}$ in *minor* which in its final period changes mode to *major*. After Azucena's cantabile is finished, the piece continues as a *parlante* mixed with song [*canto*], up until the *cabaletta*."

23. In a famous, much reprinted essay from the mid-1960s, Luigi Dallapiccola identified exact midpoints as a kind of *Geheimnis der Form bei Giuseppe Verdi;* the most readily available version of the essay in English is "Words and Music in Italian Nineteenth-Century Opera," in *The Verdi Companion*, ed. William Weaver and Martin Chusid (London, 1980), 193–215. The essay's rigorous structuralism may seen a little quaint now, but Dallapiccola's advocacy marked a critical point in Verdi's journey toward academic respectability. Pierluigi Petrobelli has also written about Azucena's peroration, pointing out its similarity to Leonora's "E

versi melanconici un trovator cantò," a passage from her cavatina in Act I, and suggesting that the connection "can be explained only by theories of deeply unconscious motivation." See Petrobelli, "Toward an Explanation of the Dramatic Structure of *Il trovatore*," in his *Music in the Theater: Essays on Verdi and Other Composers* (Princeton, 1994), 107.

24. There is also the fact that the melody is very close in shape to the duet cabaletta between Azucena and Manrico in Act II. This might be another promised *Geheimnis*, another possible route to meaning; however, the route is probably made more tortuous by further, equally obvious connections—to the count's *romanza* in Act I, for example. For a detailed discussion of the first set of connections here, together with a sophisticated examination of the possibilities and limitations of thinking about individual operas as possessing *tinta* (identifying color), see David Rosen, "Meter, Character, and *Tinta* in Verdi's Operas," in *Verdi's Middle Period 1849–1859: Source Studies, Analysis, and Performance Practice*, ed. Martin Chusid (Chicago, 1997), 339–92; see especially 379–90, which looks at relationships between *Il trovatore* and *La traviata*.

25. I should admit here that, when I gave this chapter as a lecture, some knowledgeable interlocutors found rather different meaning in this melody, quite possibly influenced by performances I have not imagined. One quite insistent subgroup proposed that the trills and chromaticism were much more sinister (or, perhaps better, insinuating) than I have suggested; their frame of cross-reference might, for example, embrace the octave melody that underpins the Rigoletto-Sparafucile duet in Act I of *Rigoletto*.

26. My thanks to Carolyn Abbate for the excursion into *Siegfried* and the sinister.

27. Basevi, *Studio sulle opere di Verdi*, 235. "Champagne and tears" is, of course, from Henry James's celebrated essay on Dumas fils, first published in 1896: "The play has been blown about the world at a fearful rate, but it has never lost its happy juvenility, a charm that nothing can vulgarize. It is all champagne and tears—fresh perversity, fresh credulity, fresh passion, fresh pain." The essay is collected in Henry James, *The Scenic Art: Notes on Acting and the Drama 1872–1901* (New Brunswick, 1948), 263.

28. A special word here for Brigitte Fassbaender's interpretation, conducted by Carlo Maria Giulini on DGG 413 355. Fassbaender's control of vibrato and non-vibrato entices forward the uncanny, unsettling our assumptions about where the voice comes from; and Giulini's classicizing tendencies toward the opera, elsewhere rather irritating (his cloak in the publicity shots says it all), here

ensure that the urbane orchestral melody is far enough forward to make its presence felt.

CHAPTER 3. ERSATZ DITTIES:
ADRIANA FERRARESE'S SUSANNA

1. Martin Bernheimer, "Operating Theater," *Opera News*, June, 2002; the copy I used is at www.operanews.com/archives/602.

2. As late as November 2004, Miller was still circulating this story. Here is a more lurid version, reported in London's *Guardian* newspaper on 19 November: "I differed with [Volpe] on a very minor issue. I wanted to drop two arias in *The Marriage of Figaro* that Cecilia Bartoli was supposed to sing. I said, 'It's mad to do these two arias, they're concert arias.' He said [puts on Bronx accent], 'Listen, you agreed.' I said, 'I agreed in much the same way that France agreed in 1939.' You could see a cloud of unknowing pass across his eyes, and he just said, 'Don't fuck with me.' If that was fucking with him, then I'm proud to stand up on behalf of something I thought was right."

3. *Daily Telegraph*, 18 November 1998. Thanks to Hilary Poriss for drawing my attention to this interview, and for generously sharing with me several other texts and ideas engendered by the Bartoli/Met/*Figaro* affair, discussion of which will become part of a book she plans on substitution arias in Italian opera.

4. After the spoken version of this chapter was first delivered, a Berkeleyan musicologist of the greatest conceivable eminence (with a nice show of irony but nevertheless in some earnest) put it thus: "You can do what you want with Donizetti and Verdi, but mess with Mozart and you mess with me."

5. In this sense, as Bartoli showed in her performances at the Met, the aria can indeed *also* function as an "action" piece.

6. "Un moto di gioia" appears on *Cecilia Bartoli: Mozart Portraits* (Decca 443 452-2); the timing of "Venite, inginocchiatevi" is from the complete recording of *Figaro* conducted by John Eliot Gardiner (Archiv 439 871-2).

7. Review in *Opera News*, February 1999.

8. Serie II *Bühnenwerke*. Werkgruppe 7: Arien, Szenen, Ensembles und Chöre mit Orchester (Kassel, 1967–72). Recordings of most of these pieces are assembled in a Decca boxed set entitled *The Concert Arias* (London, 455 241-2). It is important to recall, though, that the majority are not in fact "concert arias" but were intended for stage performance.

9. See Andrew Steptoe, *The Mozart-Da Ponte Operas* (Oxford, 1988), 209.

10. For information about Ferrarese (sometimes know as Ferrarese del Bene), see John A. Rice, "Rondò vocali di Salieri e Mozart," in *I vicini di Mozart*, ed. Maria Teresa Muraro (Florence, 1989), 1:185–209; Patricia Lewy Gidwitz, "Mozart's Fiordiligi: Adriana Ferrarese del Bene," *Cambridge Opera Journal* 8, no. 3 (1996): 199–214; and Dorothea Link, *The National Court Theatre in Mozart's Vienna* (Oxford, 1998).

11. See, for example, Stefan Kunze, *Mozarts Opern* (Stuttgart, 1984), 289: "then as today there were 'litigious individuals' among the singers; in no other way can one explain how, for the Viennese revival del 1789, . . . Mozart substituted this unique aria ['Venite, inginnochiatevi'] with the arietta 'Un moto di gioia,' which has nothing to do with the dramatic situation and which sounds superfluous." Hermann Abert, *W. A. Mozart*, 3rd ed. (Leipzig, 1919–21; 1955–56), quoted below in note 14, makes the same assertion about the second substitute aria, "Al desio."

12. For these points, and for a brilliant analysis of the "vocal acting" in this final part of the opera, see Alessandra Campana, "The Performance of Opera Buffa: *Le nozze di Figaro* and the Act IV Finale," in *Pensieri per un maestro*, ed. Stefano La Via and Roger Parker (Turin, 2002), 124–34, esp. 128–30. Another important discussion of the aria is in James Webster's "The Analysis of Mozart's Arias," in *Mozart Studies*, ed. Cliff Eisen (Oxford, 1991), 181–83, which also points out the "elevated" tone of the aria.

13. An interesting motive, this, in that it appears with similar woodwind colors and in a similar rhetorical position (launching a new section but not taken up by the vocal line) in Ilia's "Se il padre perdei" from Act II of *Idomeneo*. There the motive assumes a heavy burden of ambiguity, as is made clear when it is migrates to the minor mode and dark string sonority to launch Idomeneo's subsequent recitative. My thanks to Roger Moseley for pointing out the connection.

14. Abert, *W. A. Mozart*, 356.

15. Kunze, *Mozarts Opern*, 289. Even Lewy Gidwitz, who writes in praise of Ferrarese, is unimpressed by both replacement arias, describing them as "rather routine"; see Lewy Gidwitz, "Mozart's Fiordiligi," 210.

16. Webster, "The Analysis of Mozart's Arias," 182n109. His agitation about "Deh vieni" causes him to reach for language not often found in analytical prose: "the dry pizzicatos dissolve into liquid, undulating violin motifs rising into the night sky, surrounding the pleasing pain of [Susanna's] long B natural appoggiatura . . . the first moist tinglings of sexual arousal."

17. *New York Times*, 9 November 1998.

18. Letter, 19 August 1789. A second letter to his wife is more critical still: he describes another prima donna as "much better than Ferrarese;—though that's not saying much, of course"; letter, 16 April 1789. Both letters are frequently cited in the literature; I take them here from Lewy Gidwitz, "Mozart's Fiordiligi," 208 and 210.

19. The most balanced account of these circumstances, including the story of Da Ponte's and Ferrarese's eventual dismissal from Vienna, is to be found in John A. Rice, *Antonio Salieri and Viennese Opera* (Chicago, 1998), 421–500. Da Ponte's account can be found in his *Memoirs of Lorenzo Da Ponte, Mozart's Librettist*, trans Elisabeth Abbott (1929; reprint, New York, 1959), 284.

20. Webster, "The Analysis of Mozart's Arias," 183.

21. For a detailed discussion of these changes, see Alan Tyson, "Some Problems in the Text of *Le nozze di Figaro:* Did Mozart Have a Hand in Them?" *Journal of the Royal Musical Association* 112 (1987): 99–131.

22. For the early sketch of a rondo, see Tyson, "Some Problems in the Text of *Figaro*," 122–24; Daniel Heartz (with Thomas Bauman), *Mozart's Operas* (Berkeley, 1990), 151–52; and Heartz, "Mozart and Da Ponte," *The Musical Quarterly* 79 (1995): 705–7. The 1786 Concert Rondò is entitled "Ch'io mi scordi di te"—"Non temer, amato bene" (K. 505) and has an elaborate piano concertato part. It was written for Storace's farewell performances in Vienna.

23. This scene is discussed at length in Campana, "The Performance of Opera Buffa."

24. Rice, *Antonio Salieri*, 479–87.

CHAPTER 4. IN SEARCH OF VERDI

1. This chapter began, in a much shorter and differently angled form, as a contribution to a conference held in Parma, New York, and New Haven in January–February 2001, to mark the centenary of Verdi's death. Both my contribution, a "response" to a "position paper" presented by Linda and Michael Hutcheon, and their paper, "'Tutto nel mondo è burla': Rethinking Late Style in Verdi (and Wagner)," subsequently appeared in Fabrizio Della Seta, Roberta Montemorra Marvin, and Marco Marica, eds., *Verdi 2001: Atti del convegno internazionale* (Florence, 2003), 2:905–28 and 929–35.

2. Theodor Adorno, *In Search of Wagner*, trans. Rodney Livingstone (London, 1981), 57–58; first published as *Versuch über Wagner*, 1952. Adorno suggests that "composers such as Rossini and Auber even owe their reputation for wit" to

their use of a style in which "the singing voice 'declaims' in accompaniment, for example, by holding on to a note." He lets us know, however, that the custom was "borrowed from the *Spieloper.*"

3. A recent attempt to do just this is Charles Rosen's "Should We Adore Adorno?" *New York Review of Books*, 24 October 2002, 59–66; for a chorus of disapproval and Rosen's reply, see the same journal's 13 February 2003 issue, 49–50.

4. Peter J. Martin, "Over the Rainbow? On the Quest for 'the Social' in Musical Analysis," *Journal of the Royal Musical Association* 127 (2002): 132. Martin goes on (133) to categorize Adorno's brand of sociology as now outdated and discredited (quite possibly a good reason why he has remained so attractive to musicologists). As he says: "The effect of his work is rhetorical—he is saying 'hear it this way!' . . . just as a good critic or barrister would, in the context of a discourse in which many other persuasive voices are to be heard. . . . For the sociologist, it is the struggle itself which is of primary concern. Whose view will prevail? For how long? What are the alternatives? . . . the point is to establish the idea that 'meanings' are not to be found in (decontextualized) works, but are in a perpetual state of assertion, negotiation, challenge and so on."

5. Adorno, *In Search of Wagner,* 109–10.

6. For further details, see chapter 2.

7. Letter to Boito, 8 January 1881, in Marcello Conati and Mario Medici, eds., *The Verdi-Boito Correspondence*, trans. William Weaver (Chicago, 1994), 18.

8. Quoted in James Hepokoski, *Giuseppe Verdi: "Otello"* (Cambridge, 1987), 59.

9. I derive the following conclusions from James Hepokoski, *Giuseppe Verdi: "Falstaff"* (Cambridge, 1983), 35–53, in particular 38–41. Also of great help has been Hans Busch, ed. and trans., *Verdi's "Falstaff" in Letters and Contemporary Reviews* (Bloomington, 1997).

10. For a summing-up of this issue, with extensive bibliographic reference, see Hutcheon and Hutcheon, "Tutto nel mondo è burla," esp. 905–12; I have also gained much from reading Anthony Barone, "Richard Wagner's 'Parsifal' and the Theory of Late Style," *Cambridge Opera Journal* 7, no. 1 (1995): 37–54.

11. Letter to Verdi of 3 July 1889; Conati and Medici, *The Verdi-Boito Correspondence*, 140.

12. Letter to Boito, 10 September 1891; Conati and Medici, *The Verdi-Boito Correspondence*, 188.

13. Although I won't press the comparison, there are interesting resonances here with the composition of *Tristan und Isolde*, for which also, in Wagner's case by force of financial circumstance, the composer produced the full orchestral

score, which was then engraved, virtually scene by scene. As John Deathridge has suggested to me, this circumstance may account for the increasingly radical language of the opera—with no chance to look back and revise past scenes, Wagner felt himself on a juggernaut of experiment, one that led him ever onward in terms of stylistic advance. The other obvious comparison is with the final scene of *Turandot*, of which more in the next chapter.

14. And formal preludes are not in this sense an exception, in that they too were typically written at the last moment, after the rest of the opera was finished.

15. These revisions are dated and discussed at some length by Hepokoski, *Falstaff*, 68–75, who also prints a copy of the original version; the new version was probably first performed in an early revival of the opera in Rome (April 1893).

16. Letter to Giulio Ricordi, 16 March 1893; quoted in Hepokoski, *Falstaff*, 68.

17. Apologies to Anthony Powell for much of the wording here. I had better quote the original, which is from the very end of the last volume of his memoirs: "As the eighth decade gradually consumes itself, shadows lengthen, a masked and muffled figure loiters persistently at the back of the room as if waiting for a word at the most tactful moment; a presence more easily discernible than heretofore that exudes undoubted menace yet also extends persuasive charm of an enigmatic kind. . . . The presence in the corner—whose mask and domino never quite manage to keep out of sight the ivory glint of skull and bones beneath—seems to imply, even if silently, something of that once familiar cadence, harsh authoritarian knell of the drinker's passing day . . . 'Last orders, please—time, gentlemen, time.'" Anthony Powell, *The Strangers All Are Gone* (London, 1982), 194–95.

18. The "Verführung" collection is a fairly transparent chromatic alteration of the "Abendmahl" motive that starts the first act of Wagner's opera. This *Falstaff/Parsifal* connection has been noticed by several commentators, including Spike Hughes, *Famous Verdi Operas* (London, 1968), 510; and Julian Budden, *The Operas of Verdi: From "Don Carlos" to "Falstaff"* (London, 1981), 503. Budden thinks the resemblance is probably accidental, given that there is no obvious verbal clue attached to it. The coincidence is also considered by Hutcheon and Hutcheon, "Tutto nel mondo è burla," 918–19.

19. See Luigi Magnani, "L'ignoranza musicale' di Verdi e la biblioteca di Sant'Agata," in *Atti del IIIo congresso internazionale di studi verdiani* (Parma, 1974), 253.

20. First published in *Le Figaro*, 5 April 1894; reprinted in Marcello Conati, *Interviews and Encounters with Verdi* (London, 1984), 256.

21. Conati, *Interviews and Encounters*, 214–15. Destranges was an ardent Wagnerian, so much so that he considered only *Aida, Otello,* and *Falstaff* (works written under the influence of Wagner) would survive. This possibly accounts for the gloss put on Verdi's two words, which the interviewer pronounced were "uttered in the tone one uses when talking of giants such as Bach or Beethoven."

22. See the fifth chapter of my *Leonora's Last Act* (Princeton, 1997).

23. Letter to Boito, 5 July 1891, in Conati and Medici, *The Verdi-Boito Correspondence*, 184. A fuller Italian text for this and the next letter will demonstrate how unusual and fragmentary is Verdi's prose in these Wagner diatribes: "Vi restituisco *le Rêve* e vi ringrazio.—Vi sono delle buone intenzioni . . . ma di buone intenzioni, dicono, è lastricato l'Inferno! Non esistono in quest'opera né il Rec.vo parlato, né ripetizioni di parole, né *Couplets* né ritorno di motivi, né tante altre formule tanto in uso all'*Opéra Comique* specialmente! Tutto questo và bene; ma non và tanto bene che tutta l'azione sia rinchiusa e strozzata nel cerchio di tre o quattro, non dirò motivi, ma frasi orchestrali che girano e rigirano per tutta l'opera, senza il sollievo di un piccolo tratto vocale. . . . Vi è altresí in tutta l'opera un'uso continuo di note legate, il cui effetto deve essere ben monotono. Di più un'abuso spaventoso di dissonanze che vi mette voglia di gridare come Falstaff 'un breve spiraglio' d'un'accordo perfetto! Quante chiacchere!" Quoted from the Italian ed., *Carteggio Verdi-Boito* (Parma, 1978), 1:191–92.

24. Again the letter is to Boito, 10 September 1891; Conati and Medici, *The Verdi-Boito Correspondence*, 188. "Qui ci vorrebbe . . . debbo dire *motivo*, che andasse diminuendo perdendosi in un pp.mo magari con un Violino solo sul soffitto del palco scenico. Perché nò?—Se ora si mettono le orchestre in cantina, perché non si potrebbe mettere un violino nel solajo!!? . . . Se io fossi un Profeta i miei Apostoli direbbero. . . . *Oh l'idea sublime! . . . Ah ah ah ah!* Come è bello il mondo!!" Quoted from the Italian ed., *Carteggio Verdi-Boito,* 1:196. This comment of course refers to the original version of the finale, but the registral extremes are the same in both.

25. Letter to Giulio Ricordi, 10 July 1871; in Gaetano Cesari and Alessandro Luzio, eds., *I copialettere di Giuseppe Verdi* (Milan, 1913), 264 (original emphasis).

26. Letter to Giulio Ricordi, 14 February 1883; in Cesari and Luzio, *I copialettere,* 323; a facsimile is printed on the previous, unnumbered page.

27. Letter to Franco Faccio, 14 July 1889; in Cesari and Luzio, *I copialettere,* 702.

28. For the sake of fairness, I should report that, even in his gloomiest hours, Verdi could sometimes see the funny side of all this. On Christmas Day 1893 he

received a panettone from the young conductor of the *Falstaff* premiere, Edoardo Mascheroni, of whom he was very fond. Mascheroni had just conducted the La Scala premiere of *Die Walküre*. Verdi wrote immediately to Giulio Ricordi: "Aahhh!!! By God! By God! By all the Gods!!! . . . With a *Walkiria* on his shoulders he thinks of panettoni?—And he doesn't think about the bolts of lightning that can hit him tomorrow?" Cited in Busch, *Verdi's "Falstaff,"* 448.

29. Hutcheon and Hutcheon, "Tutto nel mondo è burla," 915; for a much fuller account, see Linda Hutcheon, *A Theory of Parody*, 2nd ed. (New York, 1984; Chicago/Urbana, 2000).

30. I am thinking in particular of two recent publications: Emanuele Senici's "Verdi's *Falstaff* at Italy's Fin-de-Siècle," *Musical Quarterly* 85 (2001): 274–310; and Laura Basini's "Reviving the Past: Italian Music History and Verdi" (Ph.D. diss., University of California, Berkeley, 2003).

31. Bernhard Schlink, *The Reader* (New York, 1997), 179.

32. Vol. 2 of *Cosima Wagner's Diaries*, ed. Martin Gregor Dellin and Dietrich Mack, trans. Geoffrey Skelton (New York, 1980), 5 April 1878; quoted in Barone, "Richard Wagner's 'Parsifal,'" 38.

CHAPTER 5. BERIO'S *TURANDOT*: ONCE MORE THE GREAT TRADITION

1. This chapter would have turned out very differently without the help of two people. The first is Gabriele Dotto of Casa Ricordi, who generously made available to me the unpublished vocal and orchestral scores of Berio's new ending to *Turandot*. The second is Luciano Berio himself, whom I never met, but who generously responded (via Gabriele) to several questions, and who more than once voiced a lively interest in seeing what I might have to say about his authorial property. Very much aware but somewhat nervous of this composerly attention, I delayed in sending him a draft; and then, on 27 May 2003, he died suddenly in Rome, leaving the musical world, me very much included, sadly bereft.

2. Giuseppe Adami, ed., *Letters of Giacomo Puccini* (1931; New York, 1973), 311.

3. The most detailed account of the genesis and musical structure of the opera, to which I owe many details (not least the inspiration for my title) is William Ashbrook and Harold Powers, *Puccini's 'Turandot': The End of the Great Tradition* (Princeton, 1991). Further information is in Michele Girardi, *Puccini: His International Art* (Chicago, 2000), 435–87.

4. Adami, *Letters of Giacomo Puccini*, 313.

5. Eugenio Gara, ed., *Carteggi pucciniani* (Milan, 1958), 561

6. Gara, *Carteggi pucciniani*, 563.

7. Mosco Carner, *Puccini*, 2nd ed. (London 1974), 229; in the last two sentences of his biography (488), Carner reiterates the point: "It was Puccini's tragedy that, for all his wonderful gifts, his flashes of true genius, something in the deepest layer of his psyche prevented him from soaring to the empyrean, as he attempted in his last opera. What bitter irony of fate that he died over this attempt!"

8. Gara, *Carteggi pucciniani*, 563; slightly different versions of Toscanini's statement are recorded elsewhere.

9. The extent of Alfano's dilemma is suggested by his recently published letter to Mario Vivarelli: "I confess that I delayed for '25' days—exactly. . . . It's the difficult business of choosing and also creating. . . . Deciding among the manuscript materials those things that He would have left—and then return to them and make them presentable. Discard those things that He would certainly have rejected. . . . Create ex novo what doesn't exist. And not be too like Alfano!" Letter, 6 August 1925; cited in Aurora Cogliandro, "L'epistolario di Franco Alfano (1924–1954) conservato a San Remo," in *Ultimi splendori: Cilea, Giordano, Alfano*, ed. Johannes Streicher (Rome, 1999), 845.

10. For detailed examinations of the Alfano ending, ones from which the following discussion largely derives, see the two volumes mentioned in note 3, and Jürgen Maehder, "Studi sul carattere di frammento della *Turandot* di Giacomo Puccini," *Quaderni pucciniani* 2 (1985): 79–163, which contains a useful compendium of three versions of the libretto.

11. Alfano inserted one further sketch fragment at the insistence of Toscanini (Calaf's sequential passage, starting with the words "Il mio mistero" and leading to his climactic announcement "Io son Calaf, figlio di Timur!"), but did so with a seeming disregard for conventional continuity.

12. The "Diecimila anni" chorus that heralds the final tableau, for example, is in a tonal context that cannot help but sound anticlimactic in the light of previous statements.

13. See the letter to Mario Vivarelli quoted in note 9.

14. William Ashbrook, generally one of Alfano's gentler critics, tellingly describes the passage: "Puccini carefully controls gradations of instrumental resources; he holds back reserves of power, he surprises with splashes of unexpected colour. Alfano's climax starts big and monotonously continues just as big." Ashbrook, *The Operas of Puccini* (1968; reprint, Ithaca, 1985), 225.

15. I refer to Barbara Spackman's *Fascist Virilities: Rhetoric, Ideology, and Social Fantasy in Italy* (Minneapolis, 1996).

16. For the this quotation, and much more on the early reception of *Turandot*, see Alexandra Wilson, "Modernism and the Machine Woman in Puccini's *Turandot*," forthcoming in *Music and Letters*. My thanks to Dr. Wilson for giving me a copy of this important piece in advance of publication.

17. Hugh Canning, *[London] Sunday Times*, 9 June 2002, "Culture" section, 20.

18. Marco Uvietta's essay first appeared as "'È l'ora della prova': un finale Puccini-Berio per *Turandot*," *Studi musicali* 31 (2002): 395–479; an English version has appeared as "'È l'ora della prova': Berio's finale for Puccini's *Turandot*," *Cambridge Opera Journal* 16, no. 2 (2004): 187–238. My thanks to Dr. Uvietta for supplying me with a complete version of the former in advance of publication. An excellent brief introduction to the Berio ending is supplied by Andrew Porter, "Solving the Enigmas," *Opera*, June 2002, 668–72.

19. Though famously keen to keep up with developments among the avant-garde, in private he was often scathing about their achievements. He described *Salome*, for example, as a "most extraordinary, terribly cacophonous thing"; letter to Ervin Lendvai, 17 May 1906, cited in Giuseppe Pintorno, ed., *Puccini: 276 lettere inedite* (Milan, 1974), 130.

20. One such interview occurred in the Italian periodical *Giornale della musica*, February 2002.

21. From the *Giornale della musica* interview (see preceding note), cited in Porter, "Solving the Enigmas," 670.

22. The *Tristan* reference occurs in mm. 12–13.

23. As Harold Powers has pointed out to me, preceding the "Principessa di morte" music with such startling layers of musical difference might well serve further to highlight its difference; but the effect of a mediation between different worlds is nevertheless undeniable.

24. Such secure information about a composer's intention may strike readers as odd in the context of this book and its topic. However, the information in this sentence was indeed supplied to me by the composer, through the generous mediation of Gabriele Dotto.

25. Precise details about most of these references, the more obscure of which the author tells me were supplied to him by Berio himself, can be found in Uvietta, "È l'ora della prova," esp. 205–6. The "reminiscences" from *Tristan*—overwhelmingly from the prelude, but also from the opening of Act II—are fairly obvious (see, for example, m. 95, example 17); those to Mahler's

Seventh and—especially—to *Gurrelieder* are much more fleeting, if not "private" tokens of homage, to be revealed to musicologists.

26. First performed there in 1984, it was revived as recently as 2002.

CHAPTER 6. SUDDEN CHARMS:
THE PROGRESS OF AN ARIA

1. Recall the first epigraph at the start of this book, from Jerome McGann's *Byron and Romanticism* (Cambridge, 2002), 2–3.

2. For an excellent summing up of the persistence of this attitude, together with apposite quotes from Benedetto Croce, Theodor Adorno, and Hans Robert Jauss, see James Hepokoski, "Genre and Content in Mid-Century Verdi: 'Addio, del passato' (*La traviata*, Act III)," *Cambridge Opera Journal* 1, no. 3 (1989): 249–50.

3. Winton Dean and John Merrill Knapp, *Handel's Operas, 1704–1726* (Oxford, 1987), 582–84. For the critical edition, see Georg Friedrich Händel: *Rodelinda, Regina de' Longobardi*, Hallische Händel-Ausgabe, II/16 (Kassel, 2002); I am most grateful to Dr. Jones for sharing his findings with me and discussing them at length, prior to publication.

4. The production, directed by Jean-Marie Villégier, was first seen in 1998.

5. Dean and Knapp, *Handel's Operas*, 584.

6. T. J. Clark, *Farewell to an Idea: Episodes from a History of Modernism* (New Haven, 1999).

7. Extensive details of *Rodelinda* revivals, both in the eighteenth and twentieth centuries, are available in Ulrich Etscheit, *Händels 'Rodelinda': Libretto— Komposition—Rezeption* (Kassel, 1997). Etscheit has, however, virtually nothing to report about music from *Rodelinda* that was sung outside its operatic context.

8. Evidence of its circulation as "Dove sei" can be seen in a number of late eighteenth-century and early nineteenth-century publications, for example: "The Favourite Song from the Opera of Rodelinda / Composed by Mr HAN-DEL / Sung by MISS HARROP at Rauzzini and Lamottes Concert / at the Festino Hanover Square" (London, [c.1775]); copy in GB-Lb: G.170.x.(25.). As the British Library Catalogue of Printed Music demonstrates, the piece continued to appear in various nineteenth-century collections of "famous arias."

9. "Holy, Holy" was originally part of Samuel Arnold's *Redemption* (1786), an oratorio fashioned from arrangements of Handel's operatic music; for the number of editions, see again the British Library Catalogue of Printed Music. The

opening quatrain is "Holy holy / Lord God almighty / Holy holy / who was and is and is to come."

10. "HANDEL'S SONGS / EDITED BY / EBENEZER PROUT / B.A., Mus. Doc. (London, [1905]); copy in GB-Lb: G.169.e. The opening quatrain is "Where now art thou, / My own beloved one? / Come, console me; / My heart is sore!" The translator is not named, but earlier arias in the collection are translated by Nathan Haskell Dole.

11. So far as I can discover, "Art Thou Troubled" first appeared, as a solo song, in the *Novello's School Songs* collection, no.1038 (26 May 1910); copy in GB-Lb: F.280.d.; it has been very often reprinted since then, both in solo and choral versions.

12. Dean and Knapp, *Handel's Operas*, 584.

13. The present author nearly takes on the role of native informant: in my short-trousered youth I warbled my way through Rothery's version of "Die Forelle" at many a local arts festival, sometimes (if memory serves) to applause. The first verse of his neo-Schubertian English fantasy, still fixed in my mind, will demonstrate how poetic times and lexicons have changed: "I stood before a brooklet / That sparkled on its way, / And saw beneath the waters / A tiny trout at play; / As swiftly as an arrow / He darted to and fro, / The gayest of the fishes / Among the reeds below."

14. The hymn is from 1862; the biblical reference is to Matthew 11:28. Another possible resonance is to the last verse of Mendelssohn's paraphrase of Psalm 42, "As Pants the Hart": "Why, O my soul, art thou cast down within me, / Why art thou troubled and oppressed with grief? / Hope thou in God, the God of thy salvation, / Hope and thy God will surely send relief." There is more troping in the "B" section poetry, most noticeably in its opening lines ("When the welcome spring is smiling, all the earth with flow'rs beguiling, after winter's dreary reign"), which echo Goldsmith's *The Rising Village:* "Here, oft when winter's dreary terrors reign / And cold, and snow, and storm, pervade the plain."

15. It is impossible to know why this bar was omitted. It was clearly not for prosodic reasons, and the word "music" could be repeated easily, as it is later in the aria. Perhaps the Novello editors considered the five-bar phrase a bridge too far for their (mostly) amateur readership.

16. Frank Kermode, *The Uses of Error* (Cambridge, MA, 1991); my reference is to the chapter that gives the book its title.

17. Mrs. Mpola is now Deputy Director (Music) in the Department of Sport, Arts and Culture in the Eastern Cape Government, South Africa.

18. This may sound fanciful, but in a CD store in Pretoria I searched in vain for Handel recordings. Eventually an assistant put me right: a whole stack of them was indeed present, but they were grouped together in the "gospel artists" rack.

19. This recording was first released as a Decca 12″ 78 rpm (with Ferrier's most celebrated version of Gluck's "What Is Life?" on the other side) in July 1946 (K 1466). It has been reissued numerous times since. For this and further information on Ferrier's recording career, see Paul Campion, *Ferrier: A Career Recorded* (London, 1992). It is likely that "Art Thou Troubled?" was a regular part of the singer's early career in the north of England; see, for example, Maurice Leonard, *Kathleen: The Life of Kathleen Ferrier* (London, 1988), 44–45.

20. Bernhard Schlink, *The Reader* (New York, 1997), 197.

INDEX

Page references to music examples are in italic.

Text: 10/15 Janson

Display: Janson

Compositor: Sheridan Books, Inc.

Music Engraver: Rolf Wulfsberg

Printer and Binder: Sheridan Books, Inc.